HOW I FOUND **GOD**, QUIT KORN,
KICKED DRUGS, AND LIVED TO TELL MY STORY

SAVE ME FROM MYSELF

BRIAN "HEAD" WELCH

FORMER LEAD GUITARIST OF KORN

HarperOne
An Imprint of HarperCollins*Publishers*

HarperOne

I have changed the names of or used nicknames for some individuals, in order to preserve their anonymity. The goal in all cases was to protect people's privacy without damaging the integrity of the story.

Photo Insert Credits: 1, 2, 3, 4, 5, 6, 7, 9, 10, 11, 12, 14, 15, 18, 20, 23, 27 courtesy of the author; 8, Ethan Miller/Reuters/Corbis; 13, Jim Christensen/Reuters/Corbis; 16, Ethan Miller/Reuters/Corbis; 17, Kevin Winter/Getty Images; 19, Theo Wargo/WireImage.com; 21, 22, Lefteris Pitarakis/AP Photo; 24, 25, 26, 28 ©Fortitude Entertainment.

A hardcover edition of this book was published in 2007 by HarperOne, an imprint of Harper-Collins Publishers.

FIRST PAPERBACK EDITION PUBLISHED IN 2008

Designed by Kris Tobiassen

Library of Congress Cataloging-in-Publication Data is available upon request.

ISBN 978-0-06-143164-7

24 25 26 27 28 LBC 31 30 29 28 27

To my two best friends:
the Holy spirit and my daughter Jennea.
I'm forever grateful to both of you
for saving me from an early grave.

"They overcame him
by the blood of the Lamb
and by the word of their testimony"

— REVELATION 12:11

CONTENTS

Author's Note...ix

Prologue...1

PART I: TO HELL AND BACK

ONE   Life Begins in Bako..................................7

TWO   It All Comes Together 21

THREE   The Final Piece 41

FOUR   It Starts to Come Apart 63

FIVE   Life Changes.......................................83

SIX   I Fall to Pieces 105

SEVEN   . . . And Get Put Back Together 119

PART II: HEAVEN ON EARTH

EIGHT   I Go Public 147

NINE   Tongues 165

TEN   Head Hunting in India 179

ELEVEN   Into the Desert 187

TWELVE   I Go Through Hell Again.........................211

Epilogue..219

Acknowledgments 223

AUTHOR'S NOTE

My life. What a trip it's been so far. Like most people, I've had enough ups and downs in my life to drive a man crazy. Like most people, my heart has been beaten up pretty badly throughout the years by myself and by others. Like most people, many of the things that I've chased after in my life have left me feeling empty and unsatisfied.

Unlike most people, I had a childhood dream to become a rock star that came true. I was able to do what I wanted to do, go where I wanted to go, and buy what I wanted to buy. Unlike most people, I gave all this up—my music, my band, my career, everything—when I had an encounter with God. After that, all I wanted to do was focus on my future, sweeping everything from my past under the rug and moving on with my new life. Or, at least, that was my plan until a friend suggested that I write a book about my life.

At first, I didn't know how I felt about that. I didn't know if I wanted to dig up all the painful memories from my past, because they were just that: the past. As a new follower of Christ, I had been undertaking the process of crucifying my past and starting a new chapter in my life. I mean, why would I want to *relive* the past if I'm trying to forget it?

Well, I prayed about it, and after a lot of thought, I came to the conclusion that exposing all the darkness from my past would be part of my healing process. I also came to see that discussing some of the stupid things I've done might save a lot of people from going down the same roads of destruction that I traveled on.

It was with this goal of helping others that I decided to write my story, to share some of my inner demons with others, so that perhaps you or someone you know can avoid the trouble that I came to know all too well. That's my heart's intention, anyway. Don't get me wrong—my past wasn't all bad. I had some good times, but most of those always seemed to lead me into trouble.

Another reason I really wanted to write this book is to help explain to my family, friends, and fans how I came to this major decision to drop everything and follow Christ. You see, I was a master at hiding my pain and anguish from absolutely everyone. I was always the one who made everyone laugh—everyone except myself that is. I would always act like a goofball, appearing to be a normal, happy guy when I was around people. But it was all a front to cover up the internal prison that my heart was in. Behind closed doors, I was a very depressed, lost soul. As you read this book, please remember that while my outer life looked happy to the rest of the world, there were a lot of things happening inside me that no one knew about. This is the story of that inner life.

It's important to understand that I'm not trying to glamorize any of my partying past in this book—honestly, I'm just trying to be obedient to God. I really feel like God wanted me to tell my story how it happened. So that's what I did. In this book, you're going to read about a lot of darkness that went on in my life before and during the Korn years. And if it offends you, well . . . some of it *is* offensive. But it's also the truth.

You're also going to read about how God has taken every bad

thing I went through and turned it around for good. That's just what he does. I've been completely clean and sober for over two and a half years; my life has never been happier.

And if he did it for me, he'll do it for anybody.

Anyway, I hope this book touches your heart in some way.

Thanks for checking it out.

HEAD

PROLOGUE

I was at home when I heard her voice.

It was the voice of my daughter, Jennea, who was skipping around the living room and singing. There was something familiar about it that I couldn't quite place. I was too wrapped up in the sight of her jumping around the house, singing in her cute, innocent, five-year-old voice, and looking like a modern-day Shirley Temple, with her hair dangling down in curly, light-brown ringlets.

A few days earlier, we had returned from my summer 2004 tour with Korn. Jennea had not been with me for the whole summer, but she had come out with us for a couple of weeks toward the end of the tour. Jennea was (and is) the love of my life. She was always so happy, and her happiness was very contagious. Even so, having her on the road with me was always pretty difficult—not because I didn't want her there, but because being on tour with one of the world's craziest rock bands was no place for a five-year-old girl. Still, she was amazing to have around. Everyone on the tour absolutely adored Jennea, and they would all try to behave around her. Our bass player, Fieldy, made up a rule that anyone who cussed in front of Jennea had to give her a buck. It was an attempt to train us to watch our mouths around her. Everyone really tried, but a few hours after we made the rule, she had already made about fifty bucks, so I called the deal off.

I wish I could say that cussing was the worst of it, but unfortunately it was just the tip of the iceberg. I wanted Jennea to watch me play guitar every night, and so I gave her these special headphones that people use at shooting ranges to drown out all the noise. During our set, I would always try and make eye contact with her. Some of the time she would notice me looking at her and she would wave and give me a huge smile. Other times I would try to get her attention, but she would be staring into the madness going on in the crowd. In general, it was just some crazy dudes screaming the lyrics in the front row, but this was not always the case. There were some times when the madness became too much. There would be girls in the front row making out with each other, or girls with their shirts up flashing all of us in the band. It was no place for a kid to be.

Jennea's presence on the road that summer was made more complicated by the fact that 2004 had been by far the worst year of my life. I had reached my own personal gutter. Here I was, the guitarist for one of the biggest rock bands in the world, raking in millions of bucks and playing huge concerts all over the globe, but I was completely miserable. I didn't understand how a person who had everything he wanted, with millions of dollars in the bank, could be unhappy.

The thought of this made me so depressed that I turned to the only thing I knew that could comfort me: drugs. That year, I pretty much lived on beer, pills, speed, and peanut butter and jelly sandwiches. Part of me wanted to get cleaned up, but another part of me wanted to die from a drug overdose. When I was on tour that summer, I fantasized about passing out and dying while asleep on my tour bus. Then, after I was gone, everyone would miss me and feel sorry for me like they did for all those other dead rock stars. Eventually, I would snap out of those dark thoughts and think about everything and everyone I had to live for. Believe it or not, even in the state I was in, I had full custody of Jennea, so I would think about her and how much she needed me. I would think about her beautiful light-brown curly hair and her smile that could chase away all my thoughts of death. I would think about how I was a suicidal rock star single father who desperately needed help.

After the shows, I would try to hang out with her and be normal, but it was hard because of my addictions. I tried not to do drugs while she was around, yet I needed them to function. So I would sneak off somewhere to snort a line of meth, or wait until she fell asleep to do it; I was a complete prisoner of the drug. The only positive thing was this: When Jennea was with me, I didn't think about dying.

Sitting at home that day and listening to her singing, I was thinking about how amazing she was. I was thinking about how she was the cutest person in the world, and how hard it would be to leave her to go back on tour that fall.

Then I heard what she was singing.

It was a Korn song called "A.D.I.D.A.S.," which stands for "All Day I Dream About Sex." These words were coming out of my five-year-old little girl's mouth, and I knew right then that something had to change. That was the moment when I started seriously considering leaving Korn, but even then, I knew considering such a move was a lot different from actually doing it. I really didn't want to leave. Since I was a kid, I had dreamed about becoming a rock star, and it seemed to me that quitting Korn also meant quitting on my childhood dream.

But then I wondered how I could stay in the band when I was so miserable most of the time. I wasn't sure what I wanted to do or what I should do; I just knew something had to change, and I had to figure it out fast. The only problem was that the drugs had messed me up so badly I couldn't make any rational decisions. When I left for our fall tour, I started doing a lot more drugs, and the suicidal thoughts started getting stronger. Death really seemed like a good option to me sometimes. I would think, *You're a loser. You're never going to be able to quit drugs. You're no good for Jennea. She's better off without you.*

I really started to believe those thoughts. I had heard stories about people dying when they mixed uppers and downers together, and that's what I was doing almost every day. I would do speed during the day, and take Xanax at night. Some nights I would go to sleep hoping I wouldn't wake up. Other nights I would go to sleep scared, hoping that I wouldn't die. I was completely out of my mind.

What went wrong with me? How did I get to this point? How did I even get out of this alive?

Well, that's the roller-coaster ride we're about to take. All the way to hell and back.

PART I

TO HELL AND BACK

ONE

LIFE BEGINS IN BAKO

I grew up in a southern California town called Bakersfield, about an hour and a half from Los Angeles. In the past few years, the place has grown a ton, but when I was younger, it was still pretty small. There are two important things that you should know about Bakersfield when I was younger:

> It was hot (we pretty much baked in the heat every summer, so we started calling it "Bako").

> There wasn't much to do.

My childhood there was pretty typical. Like a lot of kids in Bako, I grew up in a nice enough house, with nice enough parents. We were pretty much a typical middle-class family of the eighties, living at the end of a cul-de-sac in a ranch-style house with a basement. The basement was everyone's favorite room. We had a home theater system down there (well, as good as home theaters got back then), huge couches, a huge pool table, a big "Asteroids" game (just like they had at the arcade), and some workout equipment. Even my dad liked hanging out down there, since that's where he had his wet bar and a little bathroom that he used every morning to get ready for work.

Because both of my parents worked a lot in order to provide for me and my older brother Geoff, there wasn't a lot of time for hugs in the house. While I knew we all loved each other, it wasn't the kind of place where everyone said it or showed it all the time. For the most part, my dad was a pretty cool guy. He coached my soccer team as well as my brother's, took us motorcycle riding, and when he was in a good mood, he made us laugh a lot.

But every now and then, he'd have these Mr. Hyde moments when he'd get kind of crazy. I don't want to sound like I grew up with some abusive father or anything, because he wasn't; when he was nice, he was really nice. But when he got angry, he got scary. Part of it had to do with his drinking; his dad was an alcoholic, and my dad drank a bit too. While my dad usually got happy when he was drunk, he definitely had his moments when his temper would flare up—even over little things. I remember a few times when my brother or I would spill a glass of milk at dinner, and he'd change into a totally different person, yelling at us with a voice full of anger, a voice that made us feel like we were going to get beatings, though he never followed through with those. A few minutes after his anger fits ended, he was usually back to normal. They were scary moments, but then they would pass.

Overall, my mom was pretty cool and laid back—more or less your standard mom. She cooked good dinners every night, helped get us ready for school in the mornings, kept the house really clean, basically your typical mom stuff. It seemed like she had it more together than anyone else in our house, but she had her issues too—just like everyone else in the world. Growing up, I felt the most love from my mom probably because she didn't have the unpredictable emotions that my dad did.

My brother Geoff is two years older than I am, and, like all brothers, he and I fought a lot when we were kids. A couple of times it was brutal, but it wasn't always that way. We also used to play games together for hours and make each other laugh. As we got older and became teenagers, we began pushing each other away in a more serious manner. In general, it wasn't personal; it was mostly that we were just into different stuff. For example, I was into heavy metal, but he was into new wave. Back then the rockers didn't get along with the new wave crowd. Geoff used to pin his jeans real tight at the bottom and his hair was long on one side of his face—down past his eye—while on the other side, it was cut short; it was the classic new wave hairdo. I would constantly make fun of him for it and for being new wave in general. One time we were arguing in our basement about something stupid, and I picked up a pool cue and whacked him with it as hard as I could. Got him good, too. I knew he was going to kill me for that, so I ran to my mom and hid behind her until he calmed down.

Even though he didn't get me that time, he usually got me back. When he was sixteen, he had this yellow Volkswagen bug that was slammed to the ground with matching yellow rims. One day I took the bus a half-hour across town to go hang out at the mall all day with one of my friends, and at the end of the day, I was tired and seriously not looking forward to another half-hour bus ride home. We saw my brother in his bug, and I asked him for a lift.

"No way!" he said. "I ain't giving a ride home to no *rocker*."

Like I said: different.

Our family moved from Los Angeles to Bako when I was in the fourth grade. My dad decided to go into business with my mom's brother, Tom, and his wife, Becky, and together they ran a Chevron truck stop in East Bakersfield, managing a staff of full-time truck mechanics, gas pumpers, and cashiers. My mom also worked with my dad at the Chevron too. Looking back on it, it was amazing that the two of them got along so well. They worked together all day, five or six days a week, then came home at night and dealt with me and Geoff. They had their problems—and we added to them—but they worked hard to make money and to make us a family.

My parents' house in East Bakersfield was a three-minute walk from my elementary school, Horace Mann Elementary, which was the oldest school building in Bako. One morning on the way to school, I met a group of kids that lived nearby and we started hanging out after school, mostly in my parents' basement because it was so tricked out. While my parents didn't love having my friends over all the time, at least that way they knew I wasn't getting into trouble. Though I managed to avoid it, East Bakersfield had a big problem with gangs. Now, before you start picturing a lot of drive-by shootings and stuff like that, these gangs weren't exactly a bunch of gun-toting bangers. They fought a lot, but it was mostly with knives and fists. I wasn't a fighter, so I picked up a guitar instead.

I became interested in music around 1980 when I was ten years old, roughly a year after we moved to Bakersfield. My parents' very good friends (and my godparents), the Honishes, were big influences on me. Frank, my godfather, was a guitar player, and they had a piano in their house that I always liked to plink on. Even then, there was something about playing music that fascinated me, so when I saw my godfather Frank play his guitar, I started getting interested in learning an instrument myself. The funny thing is that I originally wanted to play drums, but my dad talked me out of it. I remember him telling me, "You don't want to haul around a drum kit all the time." I think he just didn't want to listen to me banging on the drums all the time in his house. I guess he wasn't thinking about the alternative that I would be into heavy metal, cranking my guitar all the time.

With drums out of the question, I chose a guitar—not just any guitar, my first guitar, a Peavey Mystic. Have you ever seen one of those? If you have, you know exactly the kind of music I was into. If you haven't, go track down a picture on the Internet. It's maybe the most metal-looking guitar ever made.

My whole family was really supportive of my new obsession, and my mom even started taking me to lessons every week. After awhile, I pretty much understood what was going on with the whole guitar thing. I wasn't a metal stud or anything, but I had a good ear, so it made sense and came pretty naturally. I could hear where notes were supposed to be played, and about a year after I started playing, I began teaching myself Ted Nugent, Queen, and Journey songs. While those were fun, what made me get really psycho over playing guitar was when AC/DC's *Back In Black* album came out. I remember hearing it and thinking, "I want to be just like Angus Young!"

That's when I just dove into my guitar. Here I was, close to being a teenager, not too good with my parents but really good on this guitar— I just started playing constantly. My parents took an interest in my playing, too. Sometimes they'd come into my room and listen while I practiced. Even Geoff would take his new wave friends into my room and have me play Eddie Van Halen's solo on "Eruption." He was proud of his little rocker brother, even if he didn't want to give me any rides in his car. It was fun, just to play. From an early age, I loved playing music. Loved it.

I loved metal. Iron Maiden, Ozzy, Judas Priest, Mötley Crüe, Van

Halen—all that stuff—and I had the look to prove it. As far as looks were concerned, I was living the metal lifestyle. I had a huge collection of pins from my favorite bands, and I'd pin them on everything: shirts, hats, and my favorite jean jacket. My mom taught me how to use her sewing machine, and I even started sewing the legs of my pants to make them skintight so I could tuck them into these big, white-top tennis shoes I wore. That, plus all my metal T-shirts—I was completely devoted to metal music.

When I wasn't playing the guitar, I was watching slasher flicks. I was a big horror film fanatic, from about age twelve to age fourteen. I *loved* horror movies, all of 'em. *Friday the 13th*, *A Nightmare on Elm Street*, *Halloween*—if it had some crazy guy killing people, I watched it. I would record movies off the movie channel on TV and would watch them over and over. Of course, they were R-rated, but my parents didn't know what I was up to since I was a pretty sneaky kid. I'd stay up late every night, hanging out in my basement, watching those horror movies after everyone else had gone to bed. I liked to see people get slaughtered, and there was always a scene with a naked girl. I used to rewind the grossest scenes all the time (and the scenes with the naked girls, of course).

During the times that I wasn't playing or watching horror movies, I would hang out with my friends. I met this kid named JC, and we were kind of bad for each other. Most of the time when we hung out, we just spent the hours listening to metal music, but sometimes we'd smoke cigarettes, or roll parsley joints with brown paper bags while my parents were at work. Once in a while we smoked real weed, too.

Oddly enough, the first time I actually first tried pot was *before* we moved to Bako, when I was eight years old. Really. I knew a kid who was interested in it, and I'd go over to his house sometimes and he would have a little roach left over from his big brother. It never got out of hand, and I don't even think I got high. I guess I was too little to inhale—well, to inhale correctly, anyway—so I'm claiming a Bill Clinton smoke-out for my first time with pot. There'd be plenty of the real thing later, though.

As I got older, marijuana made occasional appearances in my life. I didn't smoke much of it in high school, mainly because when I was a freshman, I had the craziest experience with it that scared me off drugs for the next few years. I was at my friend Paul's house, when he told me his cousin had just gotten some really good weed, and now he had some of it. He showed it to me, and I could see that it had these little crystals or something in it. But the crystals didn't bug me, so I bought a couple joints, stashed them, then went home one day after school to try one of them out. My parents were at work, so I headed to the backyard by our pool, pulling up a chair, and checking the clock, just to make sure I had enough time to get baked, then get over it before Mom and Dad were home.

2:30. Perfect.

I lit up one of those crystallized joints, took a couple of hits, and put it out.

Instantly, I no longer knew where I was.

Also, I could not move.

But I was sure that my arms were melting off my body.

Since I couldn't move, I couldn't panic, which was probably a good thing, since I was so close to the pool. This went on for a couple of minutes, and it was genuinely frightening, because I just *knew* I'd lost my arms, and then how was I going to play guitar? And then I heard my dad's car pull up to the house. This was odd, him coming home so early in the afternoon, so, with some effort, I turned my head to look at the clock.

6:15? I'd been high for *four hours*? It only felt like a couple of minutes, but I had sat there, in my backyard, holding a half-smoked, unlit joint in my hand and staring at the ground for four hours straight. All while my arms were melting off. And then on top of it all, I had to go out to Sizzler that night—before the buzz had worn off—to have dinner with my family. That was a huge battle: looking them in the eye and talking to them, pretending I wasn't still high. I was so high I didn't even have the munchies, so I couldn't eat much of anything. Just faked it. It wasn't fun at all.

While that put me off drugs during my high school years, in middle school I was still trying it with JC, but mostly we just listened to metal music. We both loved metal. He played the drums and I played guitar, and we'd jam in that basement in my house, or in his garage. I don't think we ever came up with a name for our band, probably because we really didn't have a band. It was just the two of us.

Sometimes we'd steal stuff. Remember those hats in the '80s that had the long tails in the back? Like, flaps hanging down? We both really wanted one of those because we found some at the mall that had these cool Iron Maiden patches on the front. So one day, we each stole ourselves a hat. Man, we loved those hats so much, mainly because neither of us had long hair, and those tails made us look like we had some pretty kickin' mullets. Especially at night.

Drugs . . . slasher flicks . . . shoplifting . . . I was definitely heading down some wrong roads in life at an early age, but still, I managed to do

LIFE BEGINS IN BAKO

all of this without my parents catching me. I guess that was part of the thrill too, but I don't know what my dad would've done if he found out what I was up to back then. He probably would've killed me.

In truth, my dad's tendency to fly off the handle over little things really affected me at that point in my life. The anger in his voice put a fear in me that I carried around all the time, eventually becoming a fear of confrontation. Because of that fear, I'd kind of cower at school when kids would mess with me. I didn't walk around afraid all the time, but I did feel—and look—a little weak. When any of the bigger kids wanted to pick on me, I'd just let them. That fear of confrontation would kick in, and I wouldn't even defend myself. I was a wimp.

My worst memories of getting picked on were during the years when I was in middle school and junior high. My junior high was called Compton Junior High, and after school I would hang around with these two guys. They were pretty mean to me, and they used to hold me down and give me Pink Belly (that's when they smack you with an open hand until your belly turns pink) until I would cry. Or they would simply hit me until I cried. Then they would feel bad and say they were sorry, but within a week, they were doing it again.

I hated not being able to defend myself against them, but I couldn't go running to Mommy and Daddy. Though I knew Geoff had my back, I couldn't let my big brother fight all my battles either. The end result was that I was totally stuck in my own fear. Because of that paralyzing fear, I started acting out when I was alone at home. Sometimes I'd go get April, the family dog, bring her into my room, lock the door, and beat her with my fists. Now someone else was the wimp; *I* was the tough guy. I also would have all sorts of evil fantasies about getting even with those guys at school. I'd picture the three of us at school when no one was around, playing Hide and Seek. And then in my fantasy, I'd pull a knife out of my pocket and stab them until they cried, just like I did. I guess that's why I was into all those horror movies: They were fueling my evil fantasies.

I don't know why, but I continued to hang out with those two guys throughout junior high even though they picked on me. It didn't help that I was kind of little. That's where I got my nickname, by the way. Those guys said my head looked like it was too big for my body, and so they started calling me "Head." I guess it stuck. It seems funny now, but at the time it really made me sad. I walked around feeling like I looked like a big-headed freak.

Though my life during middle school was a steady routine of practicing the guitar and hanging out with the wrong crowd, I finally got sick of those guys who made fun of me and decided to do something different. The summer after my depressing junior high career ended, I met a kid named Kevin who seemed pretty cool, in a goodie-goodie sort of way. He never made fun of me or picked on me like those other two guys, so I ditched them and became best friends with him. During that summer between junior high and high school, I hung out with him a lot. We'd go ride motorcycles in the desert, or he'd come over to my house and swim, or I'd go over to his house and jump on his trampoline.

The thing with Kevin was that his family lived in this little house, just down the street from mine, but even though his house was small, his entire family got along. Maybe it was because their house was so small and they couldn't get away from each other that they learned to be close. It was just so different from my family. My family lived in a big house, and around that time we weren't getting along all that well. If someone put us in Kevin's tiny house, we probably would have killed each other. But they were always happy, always hanging out together and having a fun time, as a family. So I started hanging out there, and whenever I was there, I felt at peace. Whereas my house felt tense, his house felt really calm and relaxed. What kid *wouldn't* go hang out at a peaceful place?

There was another thing about Kevin and his family: they talked about Jesus a lot. This didn't strike me as weird, but I don't know why, since no one else I knew back then ever talked about Jesus. I don't remember Kevin's family going to church a lot—well, I never went with them, anyway, but they would still talk often about Jesus while I was around. I guess going to a church building every Sunday wasn't as important to them as having a relationship with Jesus at home. I never questioned it, or asked them more about it; it was just who they were, what they did. They were just a happy family that seemed to get along very well. That was their thing.

I didn't know anything about Christians or God or Jesus or anything. My only religious experience was when some priest sprinkled water on my head in an Episcopalian church when I was about three. When my brother and I were a little older (but still little kids—I think I was five), my mom tried to take us back to church for a few months, but we didn't really like Sunday School, and my dad didn't want to go, so that pretty much ended my religious experience. I didn't know how it all worked. I didn't know what any of this "Christian" stuff that Kevin and his family talked about meant.

Still, if all the talk about Jesus made their house a peaceful place for me to hang out, so be it, but Kevin also talked about Jesus when he was at my house. Since we lived close to each other, he'd come over to spend the night, and I'd be like, "Come on, let's watch *Friday the 13th*," and he'd just tell me about Jesus while I was watching Jason hack up a bunch a people.

That's just the way it was that summer. During those months, I didn't play my guitar nearly as much since I was too busy hanging with Kevin and his family. I still played, but it wasn't the outlet that it had been. I had a different outlet now.

Then came the fateful day that Kevin's mother laid everything out for me. I was at Kevin's house, just hanging out in the family room, talking to his mom. He had probably told her about the stuff I was into—the heavy metal and the horror movies—and she just flat-out said, "Jesus Christ is the savior of the world, and if you ask Jesus in your heart, he will save you, and come and live inside of you." Here I was, this thirteen-year-old kid with no religious or spiritual background, and this woman was telling me about some guy coming and living inside of me. I didn't understand that at all, but she explained it all so gently and with so much love, I thought I'd give it a shot, because here's what I knew: I liked these people, they were nice to me, and I felt happy when I was with them.

I didn't say anything to Kevin's mom right then, or pray with her, but that night, after I went home, I couldn't shake the idea of what she'd said. I was in the middle of my nightly routine, sitting by myself in the basement, trying to watch a horror movie, and I couldn't get her words out of my head. I just felt drawn to the idea of Jesus, and when I thought about it, I felt a peace and love inside me I'd never felt before. It wasn't an overpowering feeling and it wasn't all that strong, but still, it was there.

I was unsure if what she had said about Jesus was true. After thinking about it, I decided it was better to be safe than sorry, so just in case, I went ahead and prayed to Jesus. I went downstairs into the cramped basement bathroom that always smelled like my dad's shaving cream, and kneeling down on the tile, I said, "Jesus, will you please come into my heart?"

I felt something.

I was thirteen years old; I didn't know what I was feeling, but I definitely felt something inside me change. What was I supposed to do about that? What changed? Was I supposed to change how I lived? I didn't know what to do, and my knees were getting cold from the tile, so I got up, and pretty much went on with my life. I didn't know it at the time, but something had been set in motion in my life, something that I wouldn't experience for another twenty years or so.

About a month after that experience, my first year of high school started. I stopped hanging out at Kevin's house and drifted back into my old ways. Kevin and I ended up going in different directions, and I never told him—or his mom—about that night in the bathroom when I invited Jesus into my heart. I don't know why, exactly; I just never got around to it. By the time school started, Kevin and I were no longer really friends, and I started hanging out with some new people. I went hard back into my music, straight into metal. Just like that, I was living the life again.

TWO

IT ALL COMES TOGETHER

Within two or three years of starting high school, I was hanging out with almost all of the guys that would eventually form Korn. It would be quite a while before we became one of the biggest rock bands on the planet, but our individual experiences during our high school years played a big role in making us the band we would become.

A couple years after I stopped hanging out with Kevin, I began spending time with a guy named Reggie Arvizu who wound up being very important to my life. Reggie had gone to Compton Junior High with me, but I hadn't really been close friends with him. We were more like acquaintances in junior high, not really hanging out with each other, but talking every now and then. I used to tell him that Duran Duran was no good, and that he needed to quit listening to junk like that and get into groups like Ozzy and AC/DC.

While I was off doing my own thing in junior high, Reggie had hung out with a kid named Jonathan Davis, who I sort of knew as well. Jonathan also went to Compton, and sometimes after school, he and Reggie would hang out. Reggie had this three-wheeler ATV, and he was crazy on that thing, riding all over the place. One day when Reggie was riding around, he accidentally ran over Jonathan. Well, it depends on who's telling the story as to whether it was an accident—Jonathan always says it was intentional. Anyway, if you can call running someone down on an ATV "hanging out," then they hung out.

When high school came around, Jonathan and Reggie wound up going to Highland High School, while I went to East Bakersfield High. We lost touch for a bit, but during my sophomore year, I ran into Reggie at a party and it cemented my friendship with him. I was only fifteen, and since I couldn't drive, my mom would drop me off at this sound company on Friday nights. She thought she was dropping me off to play guitar with my friends—but I was really going to these little parties they'd throw there. I didn't play my guitar; I just drank and listened to music. It was at one of those parties that I bumped into Reggie, and since we were both rockers, we started hanging out all the time.

Not long after I started spending time with Reggie, I got my first true taste of freedom and the responsibility that comes with it. I wasn't even sixteen yet, but my dad told me that he would buy me any car I wanted as long as it cost less than $3000, was in good condition, and had low miles.

Well, my imagination started running, and I thought of how awesome I'd look in a Baja bug, with those big ol' fat tires in the back, and one of those huge, loud engines with all the pipes and stuff coming out of it. Oh, I wanted one so badly. In the end, we figured that'd eat up too much gas, so I decided against it.

I got a Toyota instead.

Now, this wasn't just *any* Toyota—it was a white automatic Celica hatchback, bought from a private seller in the newspaper. It was a good car, in good shape, and the price was right. And, the biggest deal of all—it was *mine*. One problem, though: No stereo.

It's kind of a good thing that I wasn't old enough to drive it yet, because having to drive without a stereo would've killed me. This way, I had plenty of time to work, save money, and get a stereo in there before I started driving it.

My dad's Chevron was always a go-to job for me and Geoff (and my cousins) whenever we needed money. So I talked to my dad about my need for cash, and he put me on at the Chevron to help me earn enough to buy that stereo. It went fine, too, until my hair got too long. My hair was very important to me—I'd been growing it out since I was thirteen. It wasn't just a part of my image, it was a part of *me*. It was a part of the music I listened to and played, and if I was going to be true to myself and true to my music, I had to have the hair. But it was too long for Chevron standards, and I had to go get my own job.

Although I was busy looking for a job that would pay me enough to get the stereo and let me keep my hair long, I was still in love with that car. It was parked in my parents' driveway (since I didn't have my driver's license yet), and I would take a boombox out there and just sit in it for hours, blaring metal and cleaning it up inside. It was like having another room that was just for me. My bedroom was cool, but it was in my parents' house. This room—the gray interior of the Celica—was my room, and having my own place was very important to me.

Finally, *finally*, I turned sixteen and set off to take on the world in my Celica. Or at least Bako.

Bakersfield had a few little rock bands that played around town, and Reggie was friends with all the cool rockers from those bands. Since I was friends with Reggie that pretty much made me friends with them, too. These guys were way older than we were—old enough to buy beer. We would all get together to hang out on the weekends and drink tons of beer, usually playing quarters and listening to music.

While Reggie also played guitar, the only songs he knew how to play were songs like "Freebird" and other stuff from the '70s, because his dad and Jonathan's dad used to play that type of stuff around town. He showed me some of those classics, and in return, I showed Reggie how to play more current songs. He wasn't that bad of a guitar player, actually, but he also wasn't that good. He just didn't have what it took to play in a band, so I said, "Man, you need to pick up a bass. There are less strings, and you can probably handle it better."

Now we just needed a drummer and a singer, and then we could be a full-on band. We tried out this kid named Jonny who supposedly played drums, but he couldn't keep a beat very well, so we fired him. I called up my old friend JC from middle school, he agreed, and just like that, we had all the necessary instruments for a band.

The fact that we didn't have a singer didn't stop us. I started writing songs, with lyrics and everything, so we could be ready for someone to step in and pick up the mic. We rehearsed and rehearsed and rehearsed, and finally found this older dude named Ron to come sing for us. He was pretty good, so we let him stay.

We called ourselves "Pierct." That's "pierced," but we put a "T" on the end, because . . . well . . . just because. We practiced with Ron for a few months before we all felt ready to play for someone other than ourselves. Reggie was really close friends with this older girl named Teresa, who had helped us get in good with all those beer-buying rockers. She was hot, and she had cool friends that she would let us hang out with. One of her friends was named Jan, and she was the unofficial rocker hairdresser for every band in Bakersfield. If you were in love with rocker hair, which I was, you had to have Jan take care of it for you.

Shannon was another one of Teresa's friends, and after I started driving, Teresa and Reggie hooked me up with her. I knew I was in love with Shannon on our first date. She was this hot little half-white/half-Asian chick, who I had initially seen when she was working at a fast-food burger place a few months before I asked her out. I came up to the counter and she had a look on her face that kinda said, "Well, what do you want?" as if she was really not happy to be working there. I stumbled around placing my order, thinking the whole time about how fine she was and figuring that there was no way she would go out with me. Still a couple of months later, Teresa and Reggie told me she was into me, and I got up the nerve to ask her out. She was an awesome person, and I just knew we were going to be together for a long time.

Around that time, Teresa's boyfriend had a band that was pretty popular in Bakersfield, and she got us a gig opening for them. On the day of the show, we were incredibly nervous. The house was packed and expectations were high. Still, we came through and actually did pretty well. We went out there and played our original songs, some cheesy metal stuff with stupid song titles that I got from a porno mag, like "Bad, Bad Girls" "Fantasy Lover," and "Anytime, Anyplace." The songs were terrible, but we actually sounded pretty good. The highlight of that show was our cover of U2's "Bullet the Blue Sky." The Edge has an awesome solo in that song, and I totally had it down to a T.

After that show, we were stoked to keep going, but we had a problem: Ron lived with his girlfriend and her kid, and he decided he couldn't be a rocker and a family man at the same time, so he quit the band.

And just like that the life of Pierct was over after one show.

When Ron left Pierct, Reggie, JC, and I tried to find some other guys to play with. After looking around for a bit, we lucked out by finding this band called Toy that consisted of a singer, Richard, and a guitar player, Tom. Toy had just lost their drummer and bass player and we were exactly what they were looking for. They added JC and Reggie as a replacement drummer and bass player, and then just stuck me in as a second guitar player.

That extra guitar had a great sound and everyone really liked it. We had this rehearsal studio that we jammed in, and a lot of people used to come and listen to us jam sometimes, especially Shannon. By this point, we'd been together for about a year, and the two of us were really close, even though I was an ass to her most of the time. I was so mean to her—I treated her like shit, and she didn't deserve it. One of the main reasons I was such an ass was that I was very insecure. When I was a freshman in high school my face started to break out with some pretty bad acne, making me feel really ugly. My mom took me to our family doctor, which helped contain it a bit, but I could never fully get it under control until my late twenties. It completely devastated me, causing a lot of pain and anger that I took out on Shannon because I felt that whenever she stared at me she was looking at my acne. I just couldn't accept that she was staring at me because she loved me.

So I treated her horribly until one day Shannon and I had a little scare. She was late and it scared the hell out of us.

We had been pretty sexually active by then, but she was on the pill, and I couldn't believe that she might be pregnant. I flipped. *She* flipped. But after our initial reaction, we kinda got used to the idea, and even started to like it. It brought us closer together. I got a lot mellower toward her and started treating her the way I should've been treating her all along. It was all pretty heavy stuff for a couple of kids not yet out of high school.

After about a week of uncertainty, we found out she wasn't pregnant, she was just late. It bummed us out, but we got over it quickly. Soon, we were back to the way we'd been before, and sadly I was treating her like crap once again.

I was also hanging with my newest bandmates a lot. Those Toy guys were cool. We started drinking beer (or Night Train, or St. Ides, or other harder alcohol) while we practiced, and it was quickly getting out of hand, though I was sure I had it all under control. Altogether, Toy wasn't a bad band, except for this: we played one show and then broke up.

I was so frustrated, just hoping to one day play in a band that could last for at least two gigs. Adding to my frustration was the fact that after the band broke up, JC split on us. While Reggie and I were just drinkers, JC had begun to mess around with drugs. He lost interest in playing drums and a lot of other stuff. At the time, we didn't understand it, and we thought it was stupid to be a druggie. But eventually, we would personally experience the way drugs can totally take control of lives.

So now, when it came to music, it was down to just me and Reggie.

When I was seventeen, around the time that Toy broke up, my grandmother—my dad's mom—died, and it hit my dad hard. His sporadic battles with alcohol became much worse, and after her death, he started letting the alcohol win. His drinking was getting out of hand, just like mine was—the only difference was that no one in my family knew about mine. I was a master at hiding my drinking from my parents.

When I came home from drinking, I'd time it so they weren't home, or so they wouldn't see me. I'd drench myself in cologne to cover the smell of alcohol. I did whatever I had to do to hide it. One day, I came home after school and saw that my dad had stopped by the house to pick up some papers that he'd left there. He had a glass of water sitting on the table, and I was really thirsty so I picked it up and almost took a swig.

Of vodka. Not water.

I could smell it strongly from the glass. My dad wasn't as good at hiding his drinking as I was, I guess. He snatched it out of my hand, said, "That's mine," and took off. It was then that I realized how much my dad was struggling with alcohol, but for some reason, I still didn't see that same quality in myself.

Fortunately, my mom and my dad started going to counseling, and my dad quit drinking (and smoking) in order to get straight with my mom. That was a major turning point in his life, and he started dealing with his problems the right way.

As for me, I just kept drinking. I thought it was fun, but in reality, it was how I kept all these issues I had from bugging me. Because if they bugged me, then I'd have to deal with them, and I didn't want to do that. Besides, I was on my way out of the house in about a year anyway, so I just dealt with my problems like my dad had dealt with his: I drank them away. My dad did it, and his dad had done it, so why couldn't I? At the time, I didn't understand it, but looking back, I see now that I inherited my family's disease of alcoholism. It was a family curse that disguised itself as a good time, and it was a spark that would eventually grow into an out-of-control, raging fire.

Unfortunately, I took a lot of my problems out on Shannon. I was such a horrible boyfriend to her, treating her like crap all too often. I was controlling, selfish, and usually angry with her. It was like I was turning into my dad, but much worse. I would be nice one day, and mean the next. When she and I were apart, I would think about how much I loved her, but as soon as we would spend time together she would start to get on my nerves for no apparent reason. Though I'm sure my insecurities had a lot to do with it, little things she would say or do would set me off in these anger fits, and I just couldn't control my temper no matter how hard I tried. Every weekend, I would make her drive me to parties and sit right by my side, while I got drunk and played guitar. I was so insecure that if she talked to anyone, I got jealous and took it out on her. I was a psycho, really. Looking back at it, I can't believe she put up with my attitude and my drinking for as long as she did. I really did want to love her, but I didn't know how.

While much of my anger came from drinking, insecurities, and my up-bringing, another part of it stemmed from my musical frustration. Reggie and I missed playing in a band, and we wanted to get back on track and get a band going again. We put out the word around town that we were looking for a drummer. As we waited for a response, we just partied around town with our friends.

One day Reggie checked the answering machine at his house and heard this message from what sounded like some little kid, named David Silveria, who said that he was a drummer and wanted to try out for our band. He said his mom could drop him off at our practices and then pick him up when we were done. Reggie was like, "Who's this little kid trying to be our drummer? He sounds like he's twelve." Turned out that only his *voice* sounded like a little kid, and when we spoke to him, we found out he was only a couple of years younger than us, so we decided to try him out.

When we first met up with him at the studio, I looked at him and wasn't expecting much. He looked like a cross between Prince and Stephen Pearcy, the singer for Ratt. But when he beat the drums, he blew our minds. He knew how to play metal. We had our new drummer. We didn't have a singer, though. Or a name. We were also really missing the double guitar sound that we had in Toy, which got me to thinking about adding another guitar player that I knew from high school named James Shaeffer.

I had met James not long after I parted ways with Kevin at the start of high school. James wore brown moccasin boots and had this shaggy long hair—the typical dirt head rocker look. He played acoustic guitar a bit, and he'd come over to my house to watch me jam out on my electric guitar once in a while. I showed him a few things and, I guess, inspired him to play, just like my godfather had done for me a few years earlier.

James only had an acoustic guitar, so after we'd been hanging out for a bit I sold him that Peavey Mystic, along with the amp. I bumped up the price and charged him more than what I paid, but that guitar looked awesome on him. Being from the same school and sharing a love for the guitar helped us to become good friends.

I knew that James's playing would be a great fit for our new group and it was. For a short while after that, my musical life revolved around Reggie, James, and David. We called ourselves "Russian Roulette," but we never ended up playing any shows because we never found a singer. Instead, we just rehearsed in David's mom's garage, practicing the same songs, over and over, with no vocals. It got pretty boring. We tried to write new songs, but it just wasn't happening, and we wound up giving up after a little while. Musically, we weren't clicking.

Reggie, James, and David went off together and started doing their own thing, writing songs in this style of music that I didn't really under-stand yet. They were listening to a lot of Red Hot Chili Peppers and Faith No More, so they started writing stuff like that, which I wasn't that into. I liked Faith No More's music, but I couldn't stand the singer, and I thought the Chili Peppers were just okay. I only liked the bass player, Flea. Reggie did too and that's when he started incorporating the slap bass technique in the heavy stuff they were writing, pretty much copying those two bands. Then they called up Richard from Toy, our old singer, and I have to admit—I felt left out.

I vented a lot of those and other suppressed feelings on Shannon, and after awhile, she started to turn on me. I don't know why, but when I treated her badly, it made me feel good inside, like I was scratching an itch inside me, like I felt when I was younger and I would hit April, our dog. I felt bad, but if I could make her feel worse, then I wouldn't feel as bad.

Eventually, Shannon got sick of me and started to take control of herself. The beginning of the end came one night when we got into a fight, and she started crying with her head down. I was drunk, of course, and I said, "Quit crying, you spineless jellyfish!" And that did it. That right there. Something clicked inside her, and my doom was sealed. I was no longer the aggressive one. I was no longer in control of the relationship. I couldn't control her anymore, and I could feel her starting to pull away from me.

To add to the craziness, Reggie, James, and David were talking about moving to L.A. with their singer Richard and his mom Donna to try to make something of their music. We'd all graduated from high school by then (except David was only sixteen; David's mom gave him permission to move to L.A. to pursue music since he would be living with Donna), and they just got the hunger in their hearts to be in Los Angeles and to call their band "LAPD" (it stood for "Love and Peace, Dude"). They finally decided to do it.

And then, they were gone.

It bummed me out, but I wanted to stay in Bako and try to make it work with Shannon. I loved her so much, and I regretted how I'd treated her. I just figured if I stayed around, she'd stay with me. It was looking shaky, though. She had enrolled at Bakersfield College and quickly started making new friends. I realized that she might dump me, and I started to panic. I couldn't stand to lose her *and* all my friends at the same time. But no matter how hard I tried, I couldn't shake my anger issues, and so one day, I called her up and asked her to come over.

"I can't," she said. "I'm doing homework."

I heard someone else in the background—a guy's voice I didn't recognize.

"Who's there with you?" I shouted.

"Just my friend, from school," she said. "We're just doing homework."

I slammed the phone down and ran to my car. I was going to kill whoever this "friend" was. But by the time I got there, he was gone. Shannon didn't let me inside; she just talked to me while I was standing on her porch. She told me it was over for us. That was the first time I ever felt like my heart was getting ripped out of my chest. I had never loved someone before like I loved Shannon, and I had no idea how to deal with the loss of a relationship.

It killed me.

In a way, I felt like Shannon hadn't left me; I felt like she died. One day she was there with me; the next she wanted nothing to do with me. She was gone. I was eighteen years old and had just experienced what I thought was the worst thing that I would ever face in my life. As I look back now and distinctly remember feeling those first thoughts of suicide that would become my companions later down the road. My best friends moved away, and I lost my first love. I wanted to die.

I was in a deep depression, and I spent a lot of time doing nothing in particular and hanging out at home. One day, while I was in bed, I overheard my mom talking to her sister on the phone, saying how I'd treated Shannon like crap and that she'd seen it coming all along. There are some things you just never want to hear your mom say about you when your heart is broken, even if they are true. Overhearing that phone call broke my heart even more. I learned a big lesson that day: The truth hurts, especially when it's coming out of your mom's mouth.

I guess I did a good job keeping all this stuff to myself, because it seemed that no one knew the pain I was carrying around inside. No one knew the depth of my depression. No one knew that I wanted to die. My parents just knew that I was eighteen, out of high school, and in need of a job. And they told me so. Quite a few times. And since I didn't have Chevron-approved hair, I couldn't just go work for my dad. It seemed like all my parents cared about was me getting a job, but I needed them to care about me. My heart was completely broken, and all I really wanted was for my mom and dad to just hold me and tell me everything was going to be alright. I needed their comfort and their support, but because we didn't have a lot of hugs or communication in our house, I didn't know how to ask for this. When it came to emotions, I didn't know how to speak with anybody.

I decided I was tired of the whole Bako scene, so I drove out to L.A. to visit my friends, and they instantly saw how broken-hearted I was. They knew I needed them. Well, Richard's mom, Donna, did anyway, and she asked me if I wanted to get out of Bakersfield and move in with them. It was a huge step for me to move out of my parents' house, but Donna made me feel like she cared about my broken heart, and I was drawn to her compassion. Plus I wanted to drink my pain away with all my friends. It all sounded very exciting and the whole idea gave me hope again, so I accepted the invitation. A couple days later, I went home to grab my belongings and tell my parents I was moving out.

When I arrived back at my new home in L.A., the suicidal feelings seemed to disappear immediately, probably because I started drinking every night of the week instead of just on weekends. LAPD rehearsed constantly every night, and I was hanging out with them all the time, drinking with them while they practiced in a rehearsal space they'd rented in Hollywood. During the day, we all worked for a telemarketing company, going to grocery stores, and asking people to sign up for a free vacation to Hawaii. Whomever we signed up would go on the telemarketer's list. It paid a little more than a hundred bucks a week, and most of the time we just stayed home and wrote people's names from the phone book.

Eventually they fired us from that job, but it didn't matter; Donna took care of us when we were broke. After a while though, she got sick of us living with her. What parent wouldn't get sick of living with a bunch of partying teenagers just out of high school? There were two guys living in the living room, three guys in the bedroom, and Richard's mom in the master bedroom. That lasted about a year, but when Donna had enough of everybody, she and Richard moved to Redondo Beach, while the rest of us moved to Long Beach to share the living room in James's dad's apartment.

Our routine was the same every day: sleep during the day (we didn't have jobs to go to), get drunk on malt liquor every night. We would buy a forty of St. Ides and a forty of Olde English in Hollywood, and they would just practice, playing a few shows every now and then. Sometimes we went out on Sunset Strip to pass out fliers for their shows. I never liked their music that much, but I liked hanging out with them and carrying their equipment, kinda being their roadie.

After awhile, LAPD (they had changed the meaning to "Laughing As People Die") got a record deal with XXX records, but it was hardly what anyone would call lucrative. Basically, the label gave them just enough money to make a record and nothing else. Even so, a couple of them got attitudes when they got that record deal. I remember Reggie came home drunk one night and said to me, out of the blue, "I got a record deal. What are you doing with *your* life, you loser?" It sounds funny now, but it really hurt me at the time, because we'd been best friends for so long.

Plus, it was true. I *was* a loser. And that truth hurt even more.

I had gotten over Shannon, and I was starting to get over the L.A. scene. After about a year there, everyone was starting to get on everyone else's nerves; plus, I was sick of being drunk and broke all the time. I started to think that I had to get away from these guys, especially Reggie, so I went to James and said, "Dude, I gotta leave. I gotta go back home to Bakersfield and do something." I really wanted him to talk me out of it, to say, "No, stay here, man."

Instead, he said, "All right. Later."

I had no choice but to bail back to Bako.

Chevron was out, so after I moved back, I got a job delivering pizzas for Roundtable Pizza. I moved back because I was tired of drinking with my old friends in L.A. but once I was home, I just ended up drinking with a new group of friends. Though I didn't really know what to do with my life, I did know that I wanted to do *something* with music as a career, so I went to my dad and asked him if he could help me out. He agreed, and gave me some money to go to L.A. Recording Workshop to learn recording.

So there I was. It was 1990, I was twenty years old and headed back to L.A., this time by myself. It was kind of lonely and overwhelming, being out there with no friends, but I adjusted quickly; it became a good thing for me. While I was in school, I also stopped drinking, so that was even better.

A few months later, I graduated and began looking for jobs at the many recording studios in L.A. There were jobs out there, but none of them paid anything. They all expected me to work for free as an intern before they'd hire me on as an employee, and I couldn't do that, since I needed to support myself. I had a couple of roommates, but I still had bills to pay and stuff to buy. Working for free simply wasn't an option.

In the end, I took the only paid music industry job I could find: testing drum machines and effects processors for an electronics company. I hated that job. For months, all I did, all day long, was push buttons on these machines as they came off the assembly line to make sure all the buttons lit up. Sometimes I could listen to CDs through the effects processors, but the job still sucked. It was just this dull routine: Push the button. Watch for the light. Make sure nothing sticks. Next. I worked that job for absolute minimum, didn't make hardly anything, barely made rent. My bosses were all jerks and treated all the employees like peons.

In addition to taking this job, I also took up drinking again. Once more I began to get unhappy with life, stuck in a rut, not doing music, and depressed. Again. By that point, LAPD had broken up, and all the guys had moved down to Huntington Beach to get something else going. I didn't know what they were up to, but I was just so depressed that one day I called them and asked if they were still playing together. They told me that they'd gotten another singer named Corey and were now calling themselves "Creep." They told me to come hang out and party with them.

Hanging out with those guys, drinking, and being stupid, helped me push my depression down inside me to a place where I couldn't feel it anymore, to the same place I pushed all the other pain in my life. I don't know what it was, but hanging out with them always made me feel better, so I started hanging with them more and more. It wasn't long before David asked me to move in with him and our good friend Danny.

It sounded good to me, so I quit my job testing drum machines and took off for Huntington Beach—along with fifteen drum machines I'd stolen from the company (I told myself it was okay because my bosses had mistreated me, so they deserved it). When I got to Huntington, I put ads in the newspaper to sell those drum machines for two hundred dollars each. A few of the guys sold weed for a living, so I guess I fit right in selling stolen drum machines. I wound up living on that money for months, but I never felt good about stealing them. I just did what I felt I had to do at the time.

Like a lot of the stuff I was doing, actually.

That was pretty much life for the next year. I wasn't playing music at all—just partying a lot, hanging out with my friends in Creep, getting drunk, and watching them jam at band practice. They were pretty good, but I thought they were going to need a lot of help if they were going to get anywhere in the industry.

It was around this time that I got over my fear of drugs and started trying a few new things. One of my friends sold mushrooms and acid, so I tried those. I found that I liked both, and so I added them to my drinking routine for a couple of months until I had my second big drug scare. I drank some mushroom tea one night at a friend's apartment, and almost immediately started tripping *hard*. There were a bunch of people there, and I got really paranoid that they were all out to get me. So I bolted for my car to try to drive home, but as soon as I got in, I became so paranoid that I was convinced that every car coming down the street was a SWAT team coming after me. But I wouldn't let them take *me*! No way. I was too sneaky for that. I lay down on the two front seats and stared at my stereo. Now they couldn't see me, and I would be okay.

Except for a problem: my stereo started growing. I stared and stared, and the longer I stared, the bigger it got, until it seemed like it was as big as the car. All in all, I spent a few hours in that driveway, having paranoid hallucinations the whole time. When I was finally calm enough, I decided to head home. And then I had another problem: A *real* cop started to follow me.

Well, that made me hold my breath for a little while. I drove on as calmly as I could, and after a few minutes, he turned and I started to breathe again.

So—no more drugs for me. Not for a couple of years, anyway.

Pretty soon, Danny, David, and I moved into a new place in downtown Huntington, where I lived in the front closet. I don't know if it was really supposed to be a closet, or just a small office. It must have been a closet because you couldn't fit a desk in there. It was just a tiny room with a window, a door, and enough room for a twin bed, my stereo, my guitar, and a small amp. There was about a foot of space along one wall that the bed didn't touch.

I also rigged up a bamboo partition a little bit outside, just to have a little more room, and in the bamboo, I cut a little doorway in it to make it look like an entrance. If you walked into the apartment, you'd see this big thing of bamboo, right behind the couch, with a little doorway that led to my room. Inside the bamboo was a cardboard wardrobe box from a moving company where I hung all of my clothes.

James lived down the street with his girlfriend, Bridgette, and he came over to party with us all the time. By then, Reggie had gotten married, so we only saw him at band practice. After about a year in that apartment with Danny and David, my life began to get into as dull a routine as my job testing drum machines had been: Work. Listen to the guys jam. Party. Sleep.

In 1992, at the age of twenty-two, I was done with the routine.

Once again, I got sick of being drunk and broke all the time, and once again, I decided to head back to Bako.

And once again, I called my dad for help.

"Dad, I don't want to live like this anymore. I need to do something with my life, and I was wondering if I could come work at one of your Chevron stations for you and maybe go to college or something."

"Sure, Brian. But only if you cut your hair."

"Okay."

That's how desperate I was. I had been growing my hair out for years, and I chopped it all off to go learn the family business. It looked so weird on me, too. Like Kramer from *Seinfeld*. I wish Jan could've been there. She would have done it right.

I didn't go back to Bakersfield right away, but I came up with a date for the move and got ready to head back. But then something crazy happened. Just four days before I was set to move, David asked me if I wanted to audition with Creep before I left. "Come jam with us and see if two guitars would be cool," he said. "It might be a sound we want."

It caught me off guard at first. David didn't know it, but that's secretly what I had been wanting the whole time. I had started a couple of those guys on their instruments when we were younger, and I really missed jamming with them. Now they were inviting me to play with them again, and I was so excited, I can't even tell you. It was a great feeling.

James, however, wasn't feeling so great about it. He had gotten very used to being the only guitar player, and he didn't want to give up half his control over the guitar playing. David eventually talked him into it by telling him that if it didn't sound good, we wouldn't do it.

On the night when we finally headed to their rehearsal studio for the tryout, I was so nervous. Not only was I rusty because I hadn't played in quite a while, but I didn't want to be disappointed. They were all my friends, but I had this fear that it wasn't going to work out. If they rejected me, it was going to destroy me.

The list of reasons for my nervousness kept growing: James played an Ibanez seven-string guitar, and I had never really played one of those before. My only experience was on a standard six-string guitar, which wouldn't have worked for their sound. I borrowed one of James's guitars for our jam session, and though it took me awhile to get used to the fatter neck, I adjusted quickly enough.

When we eventually jammed, it was just plain crazy. Huge. This huge, huge sound that blew us all away. It was incredible.

And everyone dug it, even James.

They asked me right there to join the band for good, and I agreed. I was excited for so many reasons. I had played well, my friends were happy, I was playing music with my friends again—it was incredible. Just like the good ol' days in Bako. We all felt like I had the ear they needed to take them to that next level, musically.

The first thing I did was call up my dad and tell him, "Thanks for the job, but I think I'm going to stay here and try this music thing for a little bit."

Despite the uncertainty of my life in L.A., I knew that staying put was the right decision. I had this emptiness inside me, a dissatisfaction that was eating at me, but I was certain that if I could become a successful musician, the emptiness would finally be filled. I didn't even realize how frustrated I had been up until then. Music was in my heart; it was what I wanted to do more than anything, and not living that dream had been killing me. Now that I was playing with my friends, life suddenly had meaning again.

THREE

THE FINAL PIECE

A few months before I joined Creep, the band met a producer named Ross Robinson, who went to a couple of their shows and really liked their sound. Ross wanted to help them, because he saw a lot of potential there, so he hooked them up with a manager named Larry.

Together, Ross and Larry did what they could to get Creep out there, even going so far as to pay for a demo to shop to record labels. The first time they went in the studio to record with Ross, I tagged along, hung out, drank beer, watched, and even participated a bit, singing backup vocals on the demo. By the time I joined the band, Ross and Larry had been shopping the demo to record labels for a few months.

Not long after they invited me into the band, I played my first show with them in L.A., and it was a total blast. It was the third live show I had ever played, and, just like I was addicted to alcohol, I was addicted to playing live. We played at this little club and there was actually a good amount of people there. Of course, a lot of those people were friends we had brought with us.

We only played about six songs, but I felt we played them about as well as we could have. Though I kept it to myself, playing live had brought up one of my major issues with the band: the lead singer, Corey. While I was excited about playing with my friends, I had problems with Corey—mainly that, although he was a great singer, he didn't have his own style or his own unique thing. With Corey fronting our band, I knew we wouldn't get out of the club scene. Corey wasn't helping his case, either. He had a big attitude problem, and he was a control freak who got angry easily. His short fuse made it difficult to work with him.

It all came out the day after that first show I played with Creep. My roommate, Danny, was really into making movies, and we were concerned with making our live shows as tight as they could be, so we had Danny come out to the show to record our performance. After the show, David, James, and I went home and watched the video. It was so cool to see ourselves on stage, jamming; I looked like a big, pulsating pile of clothes with a head on top and a guitar hanging off the middle. But performance-wise, we just weren't where we needed to be. David summed it up for all of us:

"We suck."

We watched some more, and then David said, "We're missing something. Should we get a new singer?"

I said "Yes" before he finished the word "new."

We called Reggie and told him what we thought, and after some conversation, we all agreed that Corey had to go. It wasn't long before David called him up and broke the news to him. He was bummed and we felt bad, but we knew we had to do it if we were going to go anywhere.

So there I was: I had joined my third real band, played my third real show, and lost my third real singer. But I was just happy to be jamming with my friends again, so I didn't lose hope; I knew we would find another singer.

Without a singer, our demo was no longer usable and the label shopping had to be put on hold, but that didn't mean we had to stop playing shows. Although Corey also wrote all the lyrics, we kept all the songs and just practiced them without him. We spent a few months playing gigs around Huntington Beach without a singer; sometimes, just for fun, Reggie or I sang the choruses.

We also looked all over Orange County for a singer, partying the whole way. But as James and I soon discovered, we'd been looking in all the wrong places.

One weekend James and I decided to head back to Bako for a few days to visit our families and party with some of our old friends from home.

We had no idea what we were in for.

We wound up heading to this night club called John Bryant's, and there were a few bands playing there—nothing special, just the same ol' Bako rock bands. After listening to a couple of them, James and I decided it was late and that it was time to get going. We were literally walking out the door when the last band started playing, so we stopped and headed back inside to catch one song.

The band was called "SexArt," and they had a skinny little twig for a singer, shaking with uncontrollable intensity. He was freaky. He looked like a stick figure—like a scarecrow. He was amazing to watch already, and he hadn't sung a note.

And then he sang.

James and I looked at each other, wide-eyed. This dude didn't have the best voice in the world, but the sound of it was so unique, like nothing we'd ever heard before. The rest of the band was pretty good too, but we felt they didn't have enough excitement and intensity in their music, so they didn't do this guy justice.

He was exactly what we were looking for.

We stayed for the rest of their set, and were a little bummed when we left, wishing we could have a singer like that in our band.

Turns out the singing scarecrow was Jonathan Davis, Reggie's old friend that I knew from way back in Compton Junior High. I hadn't even recognized him up on stage. When we got back to Huntington Beach, it wasn't long before we told Reggie and David about seeing Jonathan sing back in Bakersfield. Now I already told you that David was the most mature of us, but he also spoke his mind pretty plainly. He said, "Fuck it. Let's call him and tell him he needs to quit that band and move here to join our band."

David is so persistent. He's a real go-getter—he'll keep knocking until you let him in. Somehow he got Jonathan's number and gave him a call. I remember all of us piling around David, trying to listen in as he told Jonathan, "You need to come join our band, come down here and check us out. Jam with us and see what happens."

Jonathan was flattered that we were so high on him, and he already knew Reggie—how could you forget someone who ran you over with a three-wheeler? He had heard of LAPD before, too. I think he even had one of their albums. And while he thought it was cool that we wanted him to come jam with us, he wasn't sure he should.

Jonathan was an assistant at the Bakersfield coroner's office, so he worked around dead people all the time and was into some weird, freaky things. In the end, he went to a psychic to find out whether he should come jam with us. The psychic told him that it would be beneficial for him to leave Bakersfield, move to L.A., and join the band. With that advice, he drove down to L.A. to meet us at our manager Larry's office, and that meeting was a trip. Reggie and I instantly recognized Jonathan from the Compton Junior High days. His face looked the same, but he had a big mop of dreadlocks on his head. He told us about going to see the psychic and how she told him that we would all be successful one day. He actually played us the tape of the psychic's reading. I didn't know if I believed that the lady could actually tell the future, but it sure sounded good at the time.

The day after we met with Jonathan at Larry's office, we went to our studio in Anaheim to jam with him for the first time. The first song we played for Jonathan was a song that would later be called "Need To," and we could tell just from that first song that our music was blowing his mind. He instantly started trying to make up words to our music, right there on the spot. We had this tiny PA, and we couldn't really hear what he was singing, so Reggie, James, and I walked over to the speaker while we played and put our ears right next to it to hear. When we finally heard his voice on top of our music, there were ear-to-ear smiles plastered on everyone's faces. We all knew he was the perfect match before we were even done jamming.

Jonathan joined the band immediately. He quit his job at the coroner's office, grabbed his girlfriend, and they both moved in with me and David in Huntington Beach. I was trippin, because I knew it was only a matter of time before we did something big. I felt like that psychic really did know how to tell the future, and I had a lot of confidence that we would get a record deal. Our new singer was good, our music was good, and we were only getting better.

Looking all the way back to LAPD, and even Toy, to an extent, none of the bands I mentioned ever really broke up—it was really always

David, Reggie, and James with a different lead singer. And each lead singer had brought something different to their sound. Richard, the singer for LAPD, was more along the lines of Anthony from the Red Hot Chili Peppers. Corey had this Layne Staley from Alice in Chains thing happening. Jonathan was a dark, depressing, skinny scarecrow, who was loud, yet soft, and raw, real, and unique.

So each time a new lead singer had come in, the band had changed names. Add in the fact that when I joined the band, the music changed, too. And now with Jonathan the band had changed yet again.

The point is: we weren't going to call ourselves Creep anymore.

Jonathan had an immediate idea for a new name. He suggested that we call the band "Korn," and we all liked it. It sounded kinda creepy because it reminded us of that horror movie *Children of the Corn*. (Jonathan also had a gross story about the name Korn that he got from an incident with some homosexual friends in Bako, but we won't get into all that here.)

With Jonathan on board and Ross producing, we started writing entirely new songs, and it was clear from the start that Jonathan was going to bring a whole dark edge to our songwriting. His vibe was to yell about the horrible childhood that he'd lived through. Since I had my own set of issues stemming from my bully problems as a kid, and the problems with my dad, I fit right in with him on that subject, as did the rest of the band. We all felt connected in some way because most of us shared the same sort of pain when we were kids. The pain of being rejected, the pain of being picked on, the pain of not understanding our fathers' love for us. Every one of us had similar issues with our dads when we were kids. Our pain was a pain that a lot of our fans would share later on. It felt good to be angry and vent through our heavy music.

We also decided that we needed nicknames, just to be a little differ-

ent, and since we were spending so much time dwelling on our childhood, we sort of reached back to those memories to come up with
names. Three of us had nicknames that came from our friends making
fun of our bodies' goofiness. I already told you about how I came to be
called Head. Since this was the nickname I was known by for a long time
before Korn started, I was stuck with it. James has this really long pinkie
toe that made his foot look like it had a thumb on it, like a monkey's foot.
So we called him "Munky." He decided to spell it in a weird way, mainly
just to be different.

Reggie's was more complicated, as nicknames sometimes are. His
first nickname started from me and a couple of friends back in Bako
making fun of his big cheeks and big teeth by calling him "Gopher." He
obviously didn't like that, so we made up this word, "Gar," and to us it
meant "Gopher," so that's what we started calling him under our breath.
But then he found out what *that* meant. He was kinda fat back then, so
we added "-field" to the end of it and started calling him "Garfield," like
the overweight cartoon cat. Eventually, the "Gar" got dropped and we
wound up calling him "Fieldy."

Like I said: complicated.

Jonathan had a couple of nicknames, but they didn't last, and we
just called him Jonathan.

As for David, we never could land on a nickname for him. It just
didn't fit his style, his personality. He was the youngest, but he was also
the most mature. Since he wasn't a name-caller himself, it was tough to
make a name stick on him. We tried, though. When we first met him, he
had a unibrow, so we called him "Bert &Ernie" for awhile. In addition
we tried out "Du-gaga," because he used to make this funny face that
looked like Michael Dukakis, the old presidential candidate, but that

didn't work, either. We couldn't even call him "Dave" or "Davy." Eventually, we gave up and just called him David.

So there you go. Head, Fieldy, Munky, David, and Jonathan. In a band called Korn. With names like that, we *had* to be destined for greatness.

Larry, our manager, *hated* the name Korn, by the way. He was convinced that we would never get a record deal with that name and that we needed to change it. We took some time to think it over, discuss it, and we came back to him with our decision.

"Okay, Larry, we came up with another name. But if you don't like this one, we're going to use 'Korn.' "

Larry had red hair, and a nice, big, kind of animated smile; he sorta looked like Ralph Malph from *Happy Days*. He smiled that big smile and said, "Cool, what's the new name?"

"We want to call the band 'Larry' and put your face on the cover of our first album."

Larry's face turned bright red to match his hair. We laughed a little, and he joined in, and then said, "Fine, call yourselves Korn. But nobody's gonna sign you with that name."

I didn't think they would have signed us with the name "Larry" either, but whatever, at least he was wrong.

Everyone in the group devoted all of our time and efforts to succeeding. We were writing songs with Jonathan and coming up with great stuff, so it wasn't long before we had enough material to go back into the studio to cut another demo. When it was done, Ross and Larry started the whole "shopping the demo to labels" process all over again.

It was around that time when we also got our first gig. It was at a strip club in Anaheim, California. They had a band night at the club once a week, and on band night, all the bands that were playing that night would come in at sound check and draw numbers out of a pot to see what order they played in. We won the headlining slot, our show went great, and the crowd response was even better.

After that first show, I realized a miracle had taken place: For the first time in my life, my band didn't break up after the first show. Everyone was so excited. I was on a huge high about it until I overheard some of the guys talking in my living room the next day. I was standing behind my bamboo wall when I heard Fieldy tell everyone that his girlfriend at the time had said that everyone in the band looked cool on stage except for me. I guess she said that I looked weird like I didn't fit in with everyone else up there. Hearing those words crushed me big time, but since they didn't know that I was standing behind the bamboo, I didn't tell anyone what I had heard. Instead I just shoved it deep down inside of me and tried to forget it was ever said.

In between shows, we rehearsed in this space we found in Anaheim, which was pretty far away from where we all lived. We got sick of making the drive every day, so we found a new practice space in Huntington Beach called "The Underground Chicken Sound." It was owned by this dude we called "Ball Tongue," and almost immediately he began to take really good care of us. Ball Tongue went nuts for us, actually. He started setting up shows, and printing T-shirts and stickers to use as promotion to sell at the shows. With his help, we tagged the whole city of Huntington Beach with our stickers—almost every traffic sign had a Korn sticker on it. As our fan base grew over the next year, he would also rent this big bus, throw a keg on it, and charge fans, like, twenty bucks to ride with us from Huntington Beach to L.A. We called it the Korn Party Bus.

Parties were also a good way to make a bit of extra money when things were tight. Sometimes we would get low on studio rent, so to make it up, we would buy a keg, set up at Underground Chicken Sound, and charge people around twenty bucks a head to come drink beer and watch us play. Ball Tongue would pass out flyers all over town, and it wound up being a decent way to make some money.

That dude was all over the place, all the time, doing all sorts of stuff for us. He never slowed down, and with so much going on, we started wondering where he got the energy to do everything. And then a couple of us found out how he was keeping up with all of it:

Speed (meth).

It wasn't long before I was right there with him.

It started one night after band practice. I was pretty drunk, and I didn't think I would make it home. I had done speed a couple of times with some friends back in Bako, so I knew that when you snorted it, it instantly took away your drunkenness. It also takes away your sleepiness. And then it takes your mind. And your body. And your soul.

I wish I had known that then. Instead, all I knew was that I needed to sober up quickly, so I grabbed some of Ball Tongue's speed and did a line so I could drive home. That's all it took, and I was hooked. After that night, I started doing speed about three days a week.

At the time, both Munky and I had jobs delivering furniture, and we sort of alternated schedules. He worked half a week; I worked the other half. I was off Saturday through Tuesday, so I would start doing speed on Friday night, stay high pretty much all weekend long, and then stop on Monday to get ready for work. Every week. I was tweaking on speed so much I started calling my weekends "tweakends."

Amazingly I kept the whole thing to myself. Speed is such a dirty drug; I didn't want anyone else to know I was using it. Ball Tongue and I would go score some on the sly, after band practice or some other time when the rest of the guys weren't around. It went on that way for a few months, until I found out something interesting: Munky was doing speed on the days *he* was off, too.

And guess what? So was Jonathan.

We were all doing it with Ball Tongue, keeping it to ourselves and doing it in secret. We each told Ball Tongue not to mention it to anyone else, so he never told on us. He just did it with us.

Of course, once Jonathan, Munky, and I found out about each others' habits, we started doing speed together, and we got really into it. It was about that time when we came up with the name "Ball Tongue." Sometimes he would get so geeked out on speed that he couldn't talk, no matter how hard he tried. He would just sit there with his mouth open, tongue sticking out, and his tongue looked like it had a little ball on the end of it.

When we began doing speed as a group, it took us over because it jacked us up so much. We started trying to write music while we were all geeked out on speed, but a lot of the songs sounded stupid after we came down off the high and listened to them. A couple of the songs we kept though. One of them was a song called "Shoots and Ladders." Jonathan and I stayed up all night on speed coming up with that one. The lyrics were about children's nursery rhymes being evil. Another one was a song called "Helmet in the Bush." Jonathan and I wrote that song, too. Oddly enough, the lyrics were actually about being addicted to meth and asking God to help us stop.

At first snorting meth was fun, but I soon began to feel the effects of it, and my life started getting really evil. That's what the drug does. It sucks you in by making you believe you can quit at anytime, then you turn into an out-of-control monster. I would have these anger outbursts that were so violent that they scared me. Other times, I would get really confused. I had a second job delivering pizzas, and occasionally I couldn't find any of the houses. As if these problems weren't enough, I'd get paranoid to the point where I couldn't function properly.

But I wasn't the only person who was feeling the impact of the drug. Jonathan and his girlfriend started fighting a lot. All three of us got really skinny—like, unhealthy skinny—and spent too much of our time whacked out of our minds.

It was messing with all of us in ways we never could have imagined. As for me, all my drug fears from the past were coming back to me, so one day, I gathered enough willpower and strength to quit. We all did—even Ball Tongue.

I slept for two straight weeks while I came down.

At the end of those two weeks, Ball Tongue came to my apartment to get me out of bed for awhile, and he took me over to this clothing company called Soul. Soul was going to hook us up with some free clothes, which is one of the actual benefits of being in a rock band. When we walked in, I saw this cute little skater girl sitting at the front desk, answering phones. Her name was Rebekah, and the first thing I noticed about her were her big, beautiful, blue eyes. Her hair was light brown cut into a bob, and she wore these baggy skater pants that made her look kind of wild. By the way she was smiling at me, I could tell that she dug me, and before Ball Tongue and I left with our free clothes, she and I hung out and talked for a while.

For the next few days, I couldn't get this chick out of my mind. A couple weeks later, I saw her outside this club called "5902" where we played all the time, but since she wasn't twenty-one yet, she couldn't get in. I decided to hang outside with her, and we kicked it for awhile. I asked her if she wanted to go on the Korn Party Bus to a show that we had in L.A. a few nights later. She agreed, and when that night came, we really hit it off.

Looking back now, there were three things that really stuck out about Rebekah that night. The first thing was that she pulled up her skirt and flashed me, showing me her G string (that was my favorite thing). Another thing was that she told me the other band we played with was better than us. I thought it was cute because everyone else was kissing our asses, but she straight up said that our sound sucked. It said a lot about the kind of person she was. The third thing was our first kiss. Because she was a wild girl, I expected her to kiss all crazy, but our first kiss was very soft and gentle—just the way I liked them.

We started hanging out every day, and I quickly fell in love with her. She was wild, and she was kind of a spazz, so she rubbed most of my bandmates the wrong way, but she didn't care what anyone else thought about her, and neither did I. Looking back, I can see that she had me in the palm of her hand. I kept hanging out with Rebekah, and as our relationship grew, she moved into my apartment with me. At the beginning of our relationship, things were really great—especially our sex life. I did things with her that I had never done before in my life, and that was what our relationship was mostly about at first, but after a while, she started getting really weird—almost evil. She started attacking me physically, like she was an animal, and she was freaking out all the time, worrying about crazy stuff. The cute skater girl that I met at Soul had disappeared, and I had no idea why.

It didn't take me long to figure it out. She had been hanging out at her girlfriend's house a lot, and they were doing speed over there. She was acting just like I had acted when I had been on my speed binge a couple of months earlier. I confronted her about it, and though she tried to deny it, I knew the truth.

I kicked her out of the apartment. She was just too much trouble, and at that point I didn't want anything to do with anyone that did speed.

Once she was away from me, Rebekah really calmed down. I think kicking her out was a good thing that made her realize that she had a problem. She chilled out on the drugs and started pursuing me, writing me all these letters, showing up at my house, and calling me a lot. I just couldn't resist her. When she was fun, I loved being with her. And I really did love her.

So Rebekah and I hooked back up, but not as closely as before. While she still needed a place to live, I didn't trust her enough to come crash in my apartment.

Within a few months, Larry was talking to Epic/Immortal, and he was so sure we would have a deal soon that I quit my job because, along with that record deal, we would be getting a big fat advance check. Turns out I quit too early, because we didn't have a deal just yet, and I ended up having to leave my apartment because I couldn't afford it. I spent the next two weeks sleeping on Ball Tongue's couch, just waiting for that deal to go through. It finally did, and I got the shock of a lifetime: about a year after we put the band together, Korn was finally signed to a record label.

My dream was coming true. And none too soon, because I needed the money.

The band's living arrangements were always a mess. By this time, Danny, who we called Ham-Cam, had moved into an apartment with David and his girlfriend, Fieldy had gotten divorced, and Munky had broken up with his longtime girlfriend. So Fieldy, Munky, Jonathan, and I all got an apartment together and got ourselves ready to go into the studio. We each had our own room in this apartment, which was nice. Except Jonathan. He slept underneath the stairs with his girlfriend, in a closet. And this was a real closet, too—not like that tiny room I used at our old place. You couldn't even stand up in Jonathan's closet. He had to crawl in there to go to bed. Jonathan could afford a much nicer place at that point, but he wanted to live with all of us.

This was the state of things when Rebekah dropped a bomb on me: she was pregnant.

It was a huge shock and it couldn't have come at a worse time. Though my longtime dream of getting a record deal had come true, it was bittersweet for me because I knew that having a record deal meant we would have to start touring a lot. We were going to be playing way more shows than we had been playing, and what was I supposed to do with my pregnant girlfriend? I couldn't take her with me; it wouldn't have worked. And what about when the kid was born? What then? I didn't see any other way around it, so I asked Rebekah if she wanted to get an abortion. While I was the one who first raised the idea of an abortion, I made sure she knew that the decision was totally up to her. Rebekah agreed, so we made the appointment for two weeks later.

A week after we made the appointment, I headed to Indigo Ranch, a recording studio in Malibu Hills to start work on Korn's first album (called *Korn*). The idea was that Rebekah and her friend would go to the appointment, Rebekah would get the abortion, and then she would come join me at Indigo Ranch. While I was waiting for her to show up, I did a lot of drinking in the studio. We had all quit doing drugs when we first went in, and since Ross was a big, obsessed health nut, he had us all drinking wheatgrass shooters every day. Within a couple weeks, though, we started falling back into our old habits. I started using speed again, and so did Munky. Jonathan recorded most of his vocals on speed. It was really easy to fall back into it because Ball Tongue started using again, and he would drive up from Huntington Beach to drop it off to us. And of course, we were drinking the whole time.

Drinking and drugs aside, it was pretty cool to be in the studio, recording an album for a major label. Although I knew a lot about recording from my time at L.A. Recording Workshop, I didn't use any of it, and instead I just let Ross go nuts, since he seemed to have it under control. Besides, I had partying to do.

When Rebekah finally came up to the studio on the day of her appointment, she gave me another shock:

She was still pregnant.

She was unable to go through with the abortion; instead she decided to have the baby and put it up for adoption. I didn't know how to feel about her choice, but the truth was I didn't know how I felt about either abortion *or* adoption. In my mind, it was totally up to the woman, because she was the one who would carry the baby and deliver it. I thought if you got an abortion early enough, it was no big deal. (I don't feel that way now, but I was very confused about a lot of things back then.)

At the time, Rebekah was still homeless, so I let her move back in to the already crowded apartment I shared with my band. In the meantime, she got an adoption lawyer to find parents for our child.

The next nine months were crazy. For one thing, I started doing meth again because it was just everywhere and I couldn't avoid it, which automatically made things more insane than they needed to be. Also at this time, Rebekah became the mature one in our relationship. She started interviewing a bunch of different couples to find one that would be good to raise our child. She blew my mind, asking couples detailed questions about how they would bring up the child, quizzing them about love, discipline, school, sports, and other parenting issues. In the end, Rebekah chose this very nice couple who had tried unsuccessfully to have kids for years. They were very sweet, and they went to a lot of the doctor's appointments with Rebekah, which made them really happy. As things progressed, I still wasn't sure how I felt about the adoption. Because Rebekah took such a dominant role, I mostly removed myself from the responsibilities. I didn't feel like a father at all—more like her supportive buddy.

In addition, I was heavily focused on Korn. We had finished the record, and it was about to release. When Rebekah was about 7½ months pregnant, Korn hit the road for a three-week tour with Biohazard and House of Pain. At first, I loved touring, and everything that came with it—the live shows, the fans, the parties, the adventure of life on the road—the first time I actually signed an autograph was on that tour. But I was surprised to find that I had mixed emotions about the situation. It was cool, but it felt weird because even though kids were freaking out over us, I still felt like the same normal dude inside. I didn't understand what all the fuss was about.

During that first tour, Larry was still our manager, and he negotiated with the label to pay for a little tour support. They gave him a check, which he handed over to Ball Tongue to get us a Winnebago motor home for the tour. Ball Tongue was coming along as our main driver and tour manager. We knew the road was going to be hard and that we were going to be playing every night, so we made a rule for that tour to leave all the speed at home. It would only get in the way of what we were trying to do. So when we rolled out of Huntington Beach, no one had speed with them.

Or so I thought.

About an hour after we left for the tour, our label-bought Winnebago broke down on the side of the highway. Man, Ball Tongue was so stressed out about that. I was already drinking, so I thought he was hilarious, the whole situation was hilarious—and I laughed at him and made fun of the situation because of it. For a second, Ball Tongue got scary and yelled at me to shut up, and that if I didn't shut up, he would *make* me shut up.

I shut up.

Ball Tongue worked on that thing all night long, nonstop, and I started wondering where he'd gotten all the energy, but it didn't take long to figure out. A couple of guys had brought some speed and kept it on the down-low. Though I managed to stay away from it, I drank instead, spending the rest of that tour drinking with Fieldy and keeping away from the drugs.

Halfway through that tour, Ball Tongue started getting really cranky, and he spent a lot of time sleeping. I guess he had run out of speed. Sometimes when we drove to our next show, he would go to sleep in the back while one of us took the wheel. One day, while we were driving, we noticed some smoke coming from under the hood, so we pulled over just in time to see that the engine had caught on fire. A few of us tried to get Ball Tongue to snap out of it, but he just wouldn't wake up. The motor home was *on fire* and our tour manager was taking a nap. Bad news.

Everything turned out okay. No one was hurt, our gear was fine, and we put the fire out. The only casualty was that old Winnebago. We wound up scrapping the RV and renting a couple of vans to finish the tour. We all took turns driving, and after a show, we would pile in and drive all night to the next city. One night, I took the wheel at about 4:00 in the morning, and when the sun came up, I was barely awake. I remember seeing this billboard that had a picture of this cute family—a mom and a dad, watching their little children play in the sprinkler with the family dog. I looked at that billboard, and looked, and looked. Then I realized it was moving. I saw the dog jumping through the sprinkler, and I heard the kids giggling and the parents cheering them on.

And then I came to. Slamming on the brakes, I realized I had no idea where I was. I had been dreaming with my eyes open. I punched myself in the face a few times to stay awake, but after another few miles, I was clearly too tired to drive. I pulled over and made Fieldy take the wheel.

I wish that sleeping had been my biggest problem on that first tour, but the reality was that I didn't have much fun because of all the other things going on. Don't get me wrong, I did what I could to enjoy myself, but my mind kept going back home to my girlfriend.

She was going to have a baby.

My baby.

It made me nervous, but beyond that it also made me think about the adoption more than I had when I was at home. Being on the road and away from Rebekah stressed me out in a way that I had not anticipated. She was so close to her due date, and I knew she needed me there for support. In addition, I was scared and confused. For months, I had avoided thinking about the adoption, and as a result, I still didn't have a clue how I felt about the whole thing, how I would react when the baby was born, or how I would deal with any feelings that I might have. All I knew was that I really wanted to be in this band, but it wasn't as important to me as what I was dealing with. I wanted to be back home, but I couldn't. I had to stick out the tour. I'd come this far; how could I quit now?

Toward the end of the tour, we stopped in Sacramento to play with the Deftones, and it was around then that Larry had to stop being our manager. While Larry had been managing us, he had also been working for Epic Records. When we got signed, his boss found out he'd been managing us on the side, and his boss didn't like the idea of Larry's side gig, so he had to stop being our manager. (About seven years later, I ran into Larry at a record industry party, and he summed up his decision like this: "Man, did I blow it by leaving you guys.")

Not long after Larry left, someone over at Epic recommended these two managers named Jeff and Pete. After we interviewed them a few times, they seemed to be a good fit for us, so we hired them. A few years later, Jeff and Pete would go on to create a hugely successful, mega-management firm, but back then they worked out of their house—a little office in a rented house in L.A., with a few filing cabinets. As Korn grew throughout the next decade, so did they.

When we told Jeff and Pete about the motor home troubles and how a few of us had almost fallen asleep at the wheel (I wasn't the only one!), they did two things: they talked the label into getting us a tour bus; and they told us to let Ball Tongue go. He wasn't being responsible enough to manage our tour. It was a hard decision, but they were absolutely right.

When the tour was finally over, our record released, and we had a few weeks back home before we were scheduled to leave again to support our record. I was glad to be back home to be there for Rebekah, but I still didn't know how I felt about putting our baby up for adoption until I actually saw the baby face-fo-face.

Our baby girl was born at the beginning of 1995 early in the morning, and everything inside me instantly changed the moment it happened. At age 24, I was a father. I felt a wave of intense love inside of me that I had never felt before in my life and didn't even know I was capable of feeling. I instantly thought to myself, "I can't give this baby away." I remember it like it was yesterday. The hospital staff took the baby for some routine tests and procedures, and while she was gone, they started fixing Rebekah up. With the baby and Rebekah occupied, I decided to take a walk outside by myself. Outside the hospital, I found a bench and sat down, all alone, and watched the sun come up, all the while feeling like my heart had been sucked out of my chest. Tears began to pour down my cheeks. How could I let this baby go?

I panicked. Something in me was screaming that I would regret this day for the rest of my life. It was so loud that I almost ran back inside and called off the whole adoption, but then I thought about the adoptive parents. They had been waiting for a child of their own for a long time *before* they met us. They had been with us almost the whole time during the pregnancy, going to the doctor's appointments, expecting their child. They were there at the hospital, early in the morning, waiting outside to meet the new addition to their family.

Though we still had full power to cancel the adoption, we only considered it for a little while. Rebekah and I didn't talk much in the recovery room, but it was clear that we both had the same question racing through our minds: *How can we give away our own baby?* In the end, we knew our child would be better off with those nice people. Rebekah wasn't ready for that responsibility, and I was going on tour in two weeks. It just wouldn't work out.

We gave that couple our first—and *their* first—child.

A couple of hours after the baby was born, one of the nurses brought her back in to us so we could have a few minutes alone to say good-bye to her. I took her in my arms, and all the emotions I hadn't felt while Rebekah was pregnant came pouring out of me like a flood. I cried and cried. A part of me died that day. I couldn't believe I was giving away this little miracle of a child. I had signed her over to someone else to raise her. My heart couldn't take it. Before I knew it, our few minutes were up. The nurse came, took the baby, left the room, and that was it.

We were both in total shock. While we knew this would be hard, I don't think either one of us was prepared for the emotional trauma of this decision. We were devastated.

Later that night, Rebekah was discharged from the hospital, and we immediately went to a friend's house and did a ton of speed together to help deal with the pain of giving up our baby. We didn't talk much at all. We just sat there, high on meth trying deal with our broken hearts in silence. We figured the meth was just a temporary fix; it was what we needed to kill the pain at the moment, but it was a sign of things to come. We ended up staying up for a few days without any sleep. When we finally crashed, we slept for two days straight. I woke up to the sound of a huge motor running outside my apartment. It was Korn's tour bus, waiting for me to get on board so we could go hit the road for almost the next year.

With the sound of the engine in my ears, I looked at Rebekah, who was still asleep next to me. I thought about how completely devastated her heart must've been after carrying the baby for nine months and then giving her away. If I hurt as much as I did about the whole thing, I couldn't even imagine what she felt inside.

I didn't know how I could leave her there all alone, but it was time to go tour. Time to leave my girlfriend at home all alone. Time to *really* start living my childhood dream. Time to become a rock star.

fOUR

IT STARTS
TO COME APART

My career as a rock star seemed to include a lot of sleeping. When Korn left for our second tour, all I could do was sleep. As the bus pulled away from my house, I went straight to my bunk and fell asleep. I was still coming down off that speed binge, and though I got up a few times to go to the bathroom, I slept the whole three-day trip from Huntington Beach to New Orleans. Or maybe it was a five-day trip. I don't know—I was asleep.

Before I left, Rebekah and I did promise each other a few things. We promised to quit doing speed, because we knew it would just make things more complicated and make it harder to be apart. We also promised to stay faithful to each other, which is something not a lot of rock stars promise. Or, if they promise it, they don't intend to keep it.

By the time we got to New Orleans, I had some of my strength back, and so I decided to do something random. I let Fieldy shave my head into little squares. I then bleached the squares, which made my head look like a soccer ball. So, instead of just plain "Head," everyone started calling me "Soccer Ball Head."

That first night, we opened for Bad Religion, and we did not go over all that well. We started playing, and the crowd just stared at us, like, "What are these guys doing playing with an old punk band?" They didn't know what to make of our sound and style. After that show, we spent two weeks on the road with Sick of It All—another punk band that didn't really fit our vibe.

The truth, of course, was that no one fit our vibe—we were so different from everything else out there, and we played some places that were different from everything else out there. Traveling through the south, we played a lawnmower repair shop in the woods of Augusta, Georgia. They didn't have any toilets—so we had to go out to the woods and share it with the bears.

At this point, touring was pretty much what I expected it to be. All the bands we had played with attracted a lot of crazy kids who just wanted to party. Which was exactly what we wanted to do. As the tour went on, word about our show and sound started getting out, and crowds became more receptive to us. We were rocking it every night, and people were loving us.

Rebekah and I talked almost every day, and things were cool between us. We spoke about the adoption, telling each other that it was what we had to do and that the baby was better off, but we knew we were wrecked over it. I missed Rebekah a lot. After going through that intense childbirth experience with her and after feeling that deep love for the baby, I had become much more emotionally attached to Rebekah. It was a very traumatic event for us, and she was the only person I could talk to about it, since I didn't think that anyone else would understand.

When the Sick of It All tour ended, Jeff and Pete landed us a tour with Danzig and Marilyn Manson, which ended up being a huge career move for us. But on that tour things on the road got a lot darker. To be honest, it was just downright freaky. There were a lot of really young, trippy-looking Goth girls hanging around backstage all the time. And some of the guys from the other bands were into all this kinky dominatrix group sex with whips and leather. They invited us to watch them in action in their dressing rooms a couple of times, where there would be weird, freaky, kinky, off-the-wall things going on that I'd never seen before in my life.

I remember a time before one show when one of the band's roadies called the whole tour on their walkie-talkies, telling everyone to come back behind the buses to see something cool. When we got there, a roadie was urinating on some girl. For some reason, they were laughing about it, the roadie and the girl. No one else really thought it was funny. It was pointless. Just dark, dark stuff.

As for the shows themselves, those were great, and the fans were even better, but unfortunately, on that tour, we all started drinking a lot more. In addition, cocaine became a big thing for some of us, myself included. While speed was considered dirty and gross, for some reason cocaine was okay. That was our thinking, anyway. It was just a part of the whole scene of that tour.

Aside from the coke, we mostly stayed away from a lot of the craziness that was going on around us. I think all that stuff was a little too twisted for most of us in Korn, but one of us (who I won't name) did kind of join in with them once or twice on some various activities. Fortunately, that was as far as he went. Still, many of the things I saw on that tour were not part of the rock star dream I had when I was a kid.

Back in Huntington Beach, things started getting a lot darker for Rebekah too. She began using meth again, and I was worried about her. She was telling me she wasn't doing it, but I knew better. I could tell by how crazy she was acting. She flew out to see me a couple times and started attacking me physically again. One night on our tour bus, I grabbed her arm really hard and she slammed me in the nose with her fist. Blood went everywhere and I jumped in my bunk so nobody in the band would notice. I didn't want to cause a big scene. Rebekah felt horrible and cried for about a day over that incident.

I had never been in a physically abusive relationship before; however, with speed there seemed to be a first time for everything. The violence didn't happen all the time, but it did happen. Mostly, Rebekah screamed and yelled at me, saying stuff like, "How could you let me give my baby away?" Deep down, she knew that it was the right decision for the child, but unfortunately, the drugs were clouding her mind and making it hard for her to see the truth. Of course, I was a drunk who'd been messing with cocaine, so my mind was pretty cloudy, too.

After the Manson tour ended, we began our next tour with Megadeth. We had the good slot, coming on right before Megadeth every night. Since we were playing with Megadeth, a lot of the people in the crowd were older metalheads and hardcore Megadeth fans. Sometimes, they just didn't understand our music and they would yell, "You suck!" in between songs. One night we played an outdoor show, and there was a little section of water between us and the crowd, like one of those moats around castles. While we were playing, Munky felt something fly by his head really fast, and he just thought it was some random weirdness. After the song was over, he turned around and saw a knife sticking out of his amp cabinet.

I guess when I was reading about being a rock star, this stuff was in the fine print.

On that tour, we also got endorsed by Jägermeister, and the Jäger Girls would always bring us tons of free bottles of the stuff. Most of us didn't drink it, but Jonathan sure did. He drank it like it was water to the point where it actually became a problem. Jonathan was turning into an obnoxious drunk, and we all hated to be around him. He would yell at us a lot, and once he even punched Munky in the mouth for no reason. He threw up in the bus almost every night, and then he'd drink his vomit out of the toilet just to gross us out, but it wasn't funny—it was sad. We would act like we were sleeping just to avoid him.

When the Megadeth tour ended, we got some awesome news: we had landed a tour with my childhood hero and idol, Ozzy Osbourne, which was the coolest thing that had ever happened in my life until then. I mean, here was this guy that I'd grown up listening to, and now I was going to be opening for him. But better than that, it meant I got to watch him perform every night. Front row! For free!

It was awesome. I couldn't have been happier when I was on that tour, until Fieldy and Jonathan sat me down in the tour bus and said they had some bad news. It was something they had heard and thought I should know: Rebekah was cheating on me. I couldn't believe it and tried to deny it, but they knew specific details—the dude's name, all that sort of stuff. That news hurt me so much, and I started crying immediately. I had done some crazy things on the road, but I hadn't cheated on her. It just wasn't something I even wanted to do. There were a lot of women throwing themselves at us, but I managed to avoid them most of the time. When I couldn't avoid them, I never went so far as to actually cheat on my girlfriend. Besides, Rebekah and I had made an agreement to stay away from speed and be faithful to each other. I was only on the road to play music and party. I wasn't doing speed (cocaine isn't speed!), and I wasn't cheating on her (close, but not cheating!).

I guess it's pretty obvious that I was deceiving myself big time.

I began to think that I had been really stupid. What had I been thinking? How could a relationship really last when you're a rock star? How could I have expected her to be faithful to me when I was having crazy backstage parties with a bunch of girls every night? Still, I was shocked by what Fieldy and Jonathan told me, so I called the people who had told them to find out if it was true, and they told me *they* had heard it from someone else. It was one of those things. I wound up calling tons of people who might know, and I never could find anyone to tell me they had slept with her. I needed to hear it directly from Rebekah. I needed to call her. The only problem was that I couldn't find her. She wasn't home because while I was on tour, our landlord kicked us all out of our apartment. I got in touch with one of her friends, who gave me the number for where she was staying, but every time I called, no one would answer. That tour was over two months long, and I wasn't able to talk to her until the last week or two of it.

When I finally reached her, she denied all of it and had excuses for everything. And I decided to believe her. I wanted to drop it because I wanted us to move on. I wanted her story to be true, because I loved her. So we stayed together, and I told her that when I got back, she needed to pack her stuff and meet me in Redondo Beach.

After the Ozzy tour ended, Rebekah and I got a tiny little studio apartment in Redondo Beach that worked out great. We were both so sick of the drugs and sick of all the people we knew in Huntington—we just needed to leave and get away from the drama, making a promise to each other to stay off drugs. We had a new start in a new city; we weren't going to let things deteriorate again. I didn't tell anyone in the band that Rebekah and I stayed together; I didn't want to hear any crap from them about it. It was our little secret.

Though I was happy to be with her again, everything that happened while we were touring with Ozzy had taken its toll. All the stuff that went down with Rebekah while we were on the road during that tour really robbed me of the fun and excitement I'd had about playing with Ozzy. I never really got to enjoy that tour the way I thought I would because I was so stressed out and hurt, but the guys never knew it because I was a master at disguising my pain.

When the tour with Ozzy ended, we learned another thing that hurt: Jonathan's longtime girlfriend was pregnant. Rebekah and I tried our hardest to be happy for them, but it just brought back a lot of pain, forcing us to revisit a lot of the questions that we'd tried so hard to let go of. The fact that Jonathan and his girlfriend were going to keep their baby just made our own decision seem worse, and the questions about whether we made the right choice continued to haunt us.

The answers seemed really far away.

While I was living with Rebekah in Redondo, the Korn guys and I were in the process of writing our second album (*Life Is Peachy*). The guys hated Rebekah because of all the stuff she used to pull, but since I wanted to be able to bring her around the band every now and then, I made her call them and tell them that she never cheated on me. I figured that, if she really hadn't cheated on me, then she shouldn't have a problem facing the guys and telling them so. She did it, and we started hanging around with everyone again.

Once we had written enough songs for the second record, we went back to Indigo Ranch to start tracking with Ross, just like we did for our first record. And, just like we did the first time around, we started doing speed again. Rebekah even came up and did it with us. It was only a matter of time before our drug use led Rebekah and me back to being physically abusive toward each other. It just wasn't a good scene.

By this time, I was attacking her a little bit too. When she was growing up, Rebekah experienced some physical abuse in her family, so it seemed somewhat understandable for her to express her pain and anger that way. Although I wasn't brought up in a physically abusive family, I caught on pretty quickly, and the longer we were together, the more I learned to express my hurt and anger in that way too.

As for the band, I didn't really like the direction we were going, artistically. Not on that album. We wrote and recorded it in about two or three months, so we didn't make it as good as we could have. Our plan was to get the album done quickly so we could get back out on the road as soon as possible, but the quality of the record suffered a bit because of how fast we did it—not to mention the fact that we were screwing around with speed and alcohol way too much.

One of the songs from that record was "A.D.I.D.A.S.," which I would later catch my daughter Jennea singing. I didn't even show up on the day Korn wrote that song. I called in sick because I was so tired from doing speed the night before. Jonathan wrote that song because when he was a kid, all he thought about was sex all the time. Just like most boys. The video was a trip though. In the video, all of us Korn guys got into a car accident and died, then we were put in body bags and sent to the morgue. My dad got up early one morning to jog on the treadmill, turned on MTV, and saw the video; he told me afterward that it really disturbed him to see his son getting zipped up in a body bag.

By then, another one of the other guys in the band was married and expecting a child. Again, Rebekah and I tried to be as happy for them as we could, but we still couldn't stop hurting inside for giving our child away. When we got our first pictures in the mail of the baby we put up for adoption, she was so beautiful and looked so happy and healthy—but it broke our hearts all over again to see those photographs.

There wasn't much time to dwell on those feelings though, because shortly after we got the photos, Korn was off on tour again—this time to Europe, while our new record came out. (Even though we rushed *Life Is Peachy* a bit, it still entered the Billboard charts at number three, which was a surprise to all of us.) I was actually pretty excited about touring Europe. My childhood dream was finally taking me somewhere I had never been before. Once again, Rebekah and I promised each other that we would lay off the drugs while we were apart. Partying was fine, but drugs weren't; they would only make our separation even harder. Besides, I was too excited about going to Europe—I wouldn't need any drugs while I was over there.

Unfortunately, I got over my excitement pretty quickly, because as soon as I was overseas, Rebekah started pulling her disappearing acts again. I would call her at our apartment and the phone would just ring and ring. For weeks there would be no communication between us. It was just like the Ozzy tour all over again. Back then, I didn't have a cell phone, so I'd wander aimlessly around the streets of Europe for miles just to find a pay phone, and when I finally found one, it was usually in the middle of the night in California because of the time difference.

One day I called up my manager Pete and sent him over there to check on her. He knocked on the door and no one answered, so he decided to walk around to the window to see what was up. When he peered in the window, he saw exactly what I was afraid of: Two people lying in the bed. He didn't want to mess around with that scene, so he split to give me a call, and naturally, I freaked out. I couldn't believe that this was happening again. At least, this time she couldn't deny it. Pete had seen it with his own eyes, and I knew I could trust him. I knew the truth.

I called and called and called, and finally, *finally*, Rebekah answered the phone. I told her what Pete had seen, and I think I might have even threatened to kill her. Like I said—I freaked out. Of course, Rebekah denied the whole thing, saying her friend and her friend's boyfriend were staying at our house.

Hmmm . . .

"Why?" I asked.

"Because I fell asleep at their house, and they wanted to get away because there were too many people over there."

Hmmm . . .

"Where the fuck have you been?" I asked. "I've been trying to call you for weeks."

"I've been staying at their house partying a lot," she said, quickly adding, "But not with drugs." I guess she remembered our agreement.

Hmmm . . .

Hmmmmmm . . .

I decided, once again, to believe her. Deep down inside I knew the truth, but I guess I was afraid to face it because I didn't want to get my heart broken again. I wanted someone that I could love and who would love me. I wanted someone that I could come home to after months of heavy touring. As I look back now, it's very clear that I was addicted to a lot of things that were bad for me, and much in the same way, I was addicted to this abusive relationship with Rebekah.

For the next few months, we continued to tour Europe, playing shows and getting drunk every night. Living it up, European-style. Despite my suspicions about Rebekah, being away from her was still hard, but I used partying as a distraction and for the most part it worked.

When I finally came home from that tour, I was really happy to see Rebekah. I hoped that somehow things would be different for us. That hope went down the drain when I noticed a photograph on the window sill. It featured Rebekah and a bunch of people sitting on a couch in someone's living room. There was a coffee table in front of them, and when I looked closely at the picture, I could see a bunch of lines of white powder on the coffee table.

Drugs.

I had caught her in a lie, and I had the proof right there in my hands. I freaked out and immediately went to confront her. I said, "Rebekah, if you're lying to me about doing drugs, then you gotta be lying to me about cheating on me!"

And that was when I got out of hand and began to beat her up. Most of the other times that we had a physical confrontation she had started it, but now, I was the aggressor. I was the one resorting to violence to deal with my anger and my pain. I was the one who could not control myself or my emotions. I'm not proud of this behavior, and I wish that I could have done things differently, but unfortunately, I didn't. And sadly, things between us would only get worse.

After I cooled down, we made up—though I'm not entirely sure how. Rebekah insisted that she didn't know the drugs were on the table when that photograph was taken, and she continued to deny cheating on me. I told her that I believed her because I felt bad for hitting her and I just wanted to move on. I wanted to sweep everything under the rug and forget about it. So we moved on and things chilled a little bit, but not for long.

A couple months after that fight, I found a love letter addressed to her. It was from a seventeen-year-old kid, who wrote about how much Rebekah meant to him, and how he was in love with her. I was ready to kill someone that day. Literally. I'm not a fighter, but I was so angry, I didn't know what I was capable of. I wasn't drunk, but I drank every night, so I'm sure I was a little hung over, which only made the whole situation worse. She still hadn't admitted any cheating to me, but that photograph of her in front of drugs, combined with this love letter—it all seemed to confirm what I had been trying to ignore and brought back all of the anger and the pain that I'd felt from all the other incidents.

Rebekah wasn't home when I found that letter, so I waited for her at home, getting angrier by the minute. While I was waiting, I came up with the most evil plan I could think of. When she got home, I would have sex with her one last time and then beat her with a skateboard I had. When she finally came home, I acted like I loved her, we slept together, then I pulled out a skateboard that I had hidden behind me, and hit her hard with it. She was totally in shock. This was way out of character for me, so I had really caught her off guard. She had a horrified look on her face. She screamed at me. "Why are you doing this? What did I do?"

I laughed out loud, an evil laugh. I threw the letter at her. "You cheated on me! It's right here on paper! There's no fucking way can you deny it!"

But she *did* deny it. She quickly gave me the kid's name and address and told me to go ask him myself, if I didn't believe her. Off I went. I didn't know what was going to happen—I wasn't a fighter, you already know that—but I was ready to kill this kid with my bare hands. I showed up at this kid's house and knocked on the door. When he opened it, my will to kill him sort of disappeared.

He may have been seventeen, but he was bigger than I was. He was this big dude with the face of a boy. I asked him if he ever did anything with Rebekah, and he said he hadn't. He just had a big crush on her, I guess. That was such a horrible day. I turned into a complete monster. And this is the first time I've ever told anyone about it. No one knew, except for me and Rebekah.

I went home and apologized to Rebekah, and for some reason, she forgave me.

While there are a lot of things in my past that I am not proud of, this was one of the worst. It was such a dark and depressing time in our relationship. It was an all-time low for me, that's for sure. I think it shocked us both so much that we somehow pulled our relationship closer together for a while, kind of like a turning point. Things started to get better with us for a bit, though we did have a few more gutter moments along the way.

But just as things started to turn around for Rebekah and me, the road called Korn out again. This time it was for Lollapalooza, the traveling summer festival tour where we would close out our tour for *Life Is Peachy*. Snoop Dogg and Tool were both in the lineup for that tour, so there were parties every night, and the whole thing was pretty out of control. Jonathan was still drinking a bunch and acting crazy as usual—he would get wasted and end up doing some crazy stuff. The singer for Tool, a guy named Mainard, never really hung out with any of the other bands on that tour, so Jonathan would get drunk and sit outside Tool's dressing room like a stalker and wait for Mainard to come out so they could hang out together. Eventually he won Mainard over, but together they were a strange pair.

On that tour, Fieldy, Munky, and I hung out a lot. Our favorite thing to do was get drunk with Snoop and his boys. Those guys were a trip. Snoop had a huge entourage of dudes with him and they always had a bunch of strippers hanging out with them. Almost every night, they would have crazy parties with all kinds of alcohol and food like fried chicken and macaroni and cheese in their dressing room. Their buses always wound up leaving before ours would, so Fieldy, Munky, and I would always eat their leftovers.

In addition, we spent a lot of time hanging out with the large groups of pretty girls who clung to our buses and tried to get inside. Personally, I always liked chilling with the Korn guys the most, because when there were girls around, I would always feel pressured or tempted to cheat on Rebekah—especially since the girls were so willing to do anything and were always running around the tour buses naked. A couple of the other guys in the band liked to throw girls my way because they knew I would never go after them myself, and once or twice on that tour, I found myself in the back room of my bus with a girl that they had set me up with. Although I tried to avoid it, that tour was when I came the closest to actually cheating on Rebekah. To most people (and most importantly Rebekah) my actions would have constituted cheating, but somehow I managed to convince myself that what I was doing was just innocent, when the honest truth was that I was definitely being unfaithful. Still, for a number of reasons, I did my best to stop myself before things went too far. For one thing, I was too drunk most of the time, and for another I really didn't want to cheat on Rebekah. In addition, I knew that some of the girls we were hanging out with were underage, and I just didn't want that on my conscience.

At the time, all the stuff that went on during that tour seemed pretty fun, until one night on the road when Munky started screaming at the top of his lungs and throwing up and stuff. It freaked me out, because his bunk was right across from mine. He was just yelling, "Someone fucking kill me!" He was in serious pain.

The first thing I thought was that it was from eating Snoop's old chicken and mac and cheese, but after a while, it was clear that something was seriously wrong. A couple of doctors came out to us and tried to help him out, but they couldn't figure out what was wrong with him. It killed us to see him hurting like that.

We finally got him to a hospital and found out he had viral meningitis. We got that news and found out that it would be a while before he recovered, so we dropped out of Lollapalooza. We had completed about half of the tour dates, but we decided we didn't want to go on without him. It was a hard time for us, mainly because we hated to see our brother suffer.

After Lollapalooza, we all went home and chilled for awhile until Munky was fully recovered. It felt good to relax, but as soon as he got better, it was time for us to make our next album (*Follow The Leader*). This was our third record, and we knew going in that we had to step up in our writing, and get to the next level, so we approached it with a totally different mindset than we had with *Life Is Peachy*. We were going to take our time and make it as good as it could be. Fortunately, the studio where we wrote that album was in Redondo Beach, so I had much less of a drive than the other guys, who were all coming from either Huntington Beach or L.A. While recording that album, we all worked incredibly hard to focus our attention and write good, quality songs. Sometimes we stayed in the studio for eight hours a day, writing awesome stuff. Sometimes we stayed there longer and came up with nothing. Those days were very discouraging, but still, we kept at it.

One of the main things we wanted to do was reinvent our sound, so Munky and I started messing around a lot more with guitar effects, trying to come up with interesting sounds that would help expand what Korn was all about. Because we were so serious about our writing, we stayed mostly sober in the studio during the day, since it seemed like we got a lot more accomplished when we were sober. But when the sun went down, like clockwork, we started partying.

Our writing process went kinda like this: We would lock ourselves in a room for hours and hours, jamming until someone came up with something cool. Sometimes it would be David coming up with a cool beat. Other times it was me or Munky or Fieldy coming up with a cool riff. Jonathan even came up with some really cool riffs. Once we had the music down, Jonathan would write all of the lyrics. I remember on one song called "Got the Life," after Jonathan wrote the lyrics, we all knew it would be a big single. It had this cool disco beat to it, and the lyrics seemed really cool at the time:

"God paged me / you'll never see the light / who wants to see? / God told me / you already got the life / Oh, I see."

We could tell that the song was going to be big and it was. When it came time to record the video for it, we used this director named McG. He had done our first video ever, "Blind," which we liked, so we decided to use him again for "Got the Life." The video was split into three segments. First, Jonathan gets pestered by a bunch of paparazzi, and he ends up smashing their cameras with a baseball bat. Then after that Reggie and I give our expensive car away to a bum (who was played by a rapper friend of ours named Tre from the Pharcyde), and finally Munky and

David drive their car off of a cliff and it blows up. (I gotta admit—it was kind of fun to blow up a car in that video.)

On that album, there was another good song that was also pretty freaky. It was a song called "My Gift To You." At the time, Jonathan was having trouble with his girlfriend, so he wrote these freaky lyrics about strangling her to death, and having sex with her dead corpse. At first, the rest of us weren't too sure about those words, but we ended up loving them because they were crazy lyrics and we were a crazy band. The huge single from that album was called "Freak on a Leash." It was about Jonathan being a freak on a leash—sort of a kinky dominatrix thing.

The song became a huge hit, which probably had something to do with the fact that the video for it was out of control. It was our highest-budget video because of all the visual effects and animation that were in it. The coolest thing about that video was that we wound up winning some MTV video music awards and a couple of Grammy awards too.

Another disturbing song on that album was called "Pretty," which was about Jonathan's old job at the Bakersfield coroner's office. When he had that job, he used to have to go tell people that their loved ones had died, and sometimes he even had to go pick up the dead bodies at the accident scene and take them to the morgue. "Pretty" was about one time when he had to pick up a dead baby off of a public bathroom floor. Apparently, the baby had been raped and killed, and the song was about how hard it had been for him to see that kind of horror.

Jonathan also has a really mellow side to him that I loved a lot. While a lot of his lyrics were a little hard for some people to take, he's a really nice, down-to-earth guy. There was a song, called "Seed," that he wrote on *Follow the Leader*, which brought out that side of him too. It was about the love he has for his son, Nathan, and the song really meant a lot to him.

Anyway, when the songs had been written and it was time to record, our daytime sobriety came to an abrupt halt. We started recording in this north Hollywood studio, and while we were there, things turned pretty crazy. During our sessions there, we spent thousands of dollars on alcohol. But we weren't the only ones doing the drinking—we had a bunch of new Hollywood friends that we hung out with, mostly other musicians or people in the porn industry.

From all that partying and recording, I learned something interesting about the porn industry—mainly that it's very similar to the music industry. For one thing, it's all about money, and for another, most of the people in it are depressed druggies and alcoholics. As a result, we had a lot in common with many of those porn stars. In spite of the similarities, whenever I was around those porn industry people, I always sensed a strong, dark, depressing feeling in the air that freaked me out a bit. It made me want to just do my guitar tracks and split, which is basically what I did, since Rebekah was getting very jealous by then and it was better if I didn't spend too much time there.

That's when I picked up another bad habit—like I needed a new one. I started driving home drunk from the studio every night. At that point, I had a new car, and I figured the cops wouldn't pull me over because I looked like a classy citizen. I really made an attempt not to swerve or anything like that—especially because I always had an open container in my lap. Looking back on that, I'm so thankful that I didn't hurt anyone or hurt myself. I don't know how I didn't get pulled over or get into an accident during those days, but somehow I survived the bad decisions.

Despite the partying and the porn, we still managed to create a record that we were really proud of. All the crazy stuff from the recording process couldn't distract us from the solid focus that we'd achieved while writing. It was a good thing too, because we weren't the only people who were pleased with the record. It was playing well to everyone who listened to it and a whole lot of people were about to buy it.

fIVE

LIFE CHANGES

Until *Follow the Leader* came out, most of my rock star life was pretty fun, but with big changes on the horizon, I knew it was always important to remember that this was my job, and I had to be responsible with the money I earned. As far as money went, Korn was doing pretty well, so I decided this was the perfect time to buy my first house in Redondo Beach. It was a nice transition from apartment living. Rebekah and I lived there with her sister and her sister's daughter, and there was even enough space for a separate studio apartment under the garage that I rented out to a friend.

By that time, Rebekah and I had slipped up and done speed a few times, but on the whole, we were doing a lot better and had slowed down our using to the point where we only messed with it once in a great while. We weren't hooked, just dabbling, and that's how it went for a while. We settled into a nice routine, being mostly happy with each other, while I was off writing and recording songs for our album. Then I got a shock, for the second time in my life:

Rebekah was pregnant.

This time, we were determined to be parents, and we were so

happy. We were older (I was twenty-seven years old this time) and more stable; but more importantly, we just knew we could make it work. We figured having our own baby would cement our relationship together forever. Still, there was one hitch: I didn't really want to do the whole marriage thing because one of my worst fears in life was getting divorced and losing half my money. I mean, I loved Rebekah and all, but marriage was a big step. Besides—things were fine the way they were; why change them?

The problem though came down to money. Even though I was making decent money, I still wasn't rich. The first time that Rebekah was pregnant, the adoptive family had taken care of all the costs associated with the pregnancy—from doctors' bills to the hospital stay, they covered it all. Not surprisingly being a rock star didn't offer me health insurance at that time, and I didn't want to pay cash for all the pregnancy expenses, so I decided that I needed to get medical coverage for Rebekah. When I checked into it, I found out that insurance for Rebekah and the baby would cost a whole lot of money, but if we were married, it would be significantly cheaper.

So in a move that was probably one of my trashiest and least romantic, I decided to go ahead and marry her in the name of more affordable health care. But I really did love her, so I felt good about it. Rebekah didn't want to have an actual wedding with a minister, bridesmaids, or other traditional people, and instead we just looked through the Yellow Pages for someone to marry us. I have to admit, at the time, I liked the idea mainly because I wouldn't have to fork out thousands of dollars on a wedding. We wound up getting married at a place in a strip mall that looked like one of those stores where you could rent mailboxes and ship packages. On the day we got married in March 1998, we cried some *happy* tears for the first time ever. We decided to put off our honeymoon until after she had the baby, so there we were, husband and wife, in a nice little house, with a baby on the way. Things were going to be great.

And they were great for a while, but I always managed to mess things up a few times along the way. Like when I talked Rebekah into calling one of her friends to score me some meth. I would make my pregnant wife go and score me speed while I waited at home because I didn't like her friends. This was definitely one of my trashier moves.

After she brought it home, I would get high and stay up all night messing with my guitar or looking at some porno magazines I had hidden in our guest room. Sometimes, the day after I did the speed, I would have those familiar fits of rage. In those fits I even hurt Rebekah a few times. Sometimes I would mouth off and piss her off so bad that she would hit me first, but I would hurt her back by grabbing her real hard, making her cry, and leaving a bruise or two on her arms. Over the years, we used to joke around and call the bruises that we gave each other "love marks."

Somehow in between these episodes of mine, we managed to be pretty happy—a functioning dysfunctional couple. Though these episodes happened only a few times, I soon realized that my behavior towards my wife was totally unacceptable and I had to change fast. So a couple of months before the baby was born, I decided to get completely sober and take a totally new approach to life. I just said "no" to all drugs and alcohol and firmly committed myself to getting clean. I even started eating right and working out. It felt unbelievable, and for the first time in years, I was clear-headed. I could focus on things in a new way, and I hadn't ever felt better.

Being clean also made it all the easier for me to appreciate my daughter's birth in July. I can't even describe what life was like when my baby girl came into the world. The breath of life that happened when she entered the world was the most awesome thing. A complete miracle.

We named her "Jennea."

I was in tears. Rebekah was in tears. *Everyone* was in tears. I looked at Jennea as I held her in my arms. I was a father. I was a *father*! I couldn't believe it. It was as if some of the pain of giving up my first child was healed the second I laid eyes on her. Not that she replaced the love I felt for my first child, but I felt like I had been given a second chance to be a real father. Beyond that, it felt like Rebekah and I had a second chance at happiness together. I was just sure that adding Jennea to our family was going to encourage both of us to make responsible choices for our lives. This time, the baby was mine. She was ours. *We* were the parents—no one else. And we were going to be the best parents we could be.

Fieldy and Jonathan already had kids themselves, and when they both came up to the hospital to congratulate us, I was so proud to show them my baby. Now that we had our own kid, I felt sure that we were going to get closer to their families. Everything was going to work out perfectly.

The first night we had Jennea home, I just stared at her for hours while she slept in her crib. I couldn't believe she was real; I couldn't believe I had a baby of my own. Like a lot of new parents, I was so scared she would stop breathing because she was so little—I had heard of that happening before—I set the alarm to wake up and check on her every couple of hours. I had never changed a diaper before in my life, but I did it for her, and I didn't mind it at all. Rebekah was a great mother—she was a natural. I would worry about doing everything perfectly, and she would always calm me down. Having Jennea did wonders for us. Everything was going to be good from then on.

I held her all the time. It started the day she was born, when I just held her in my arms, looked into her little face, and thought, "She is perfect, and I never want to leave her."

A few weeks later, I had to go on tour to Japan.

Leaving my family for that tour was incredibly painful. While I was really bummed that I had to go, at the same time I was excited to go to Japan for the first time. Our first show went really well too. In fact, it went so well that I decided to have a beer to celebrate. Just one, though.

After that, I decided to have a few more.

After that, I wasn't sober anymore. Just like that, I was back to my old ways, and things went on like that for the rest of the tour.

When we got back to the States, we did this huge press campaign to promote *Follow the Leader*, and shortly thereafter, with our managers, we all came up with the idea for a tour called "The Family Values Tour." The idea was to create a tour that we could put indoors with a bunch of crazy stage props for each band—like an indoor Lollapalooza. We put a lot of other bands like Limp Bizkit and Ice Cube on that tour to open for us, and it worked. During that tour, we started selling around one hundred thousand or more copies of our album a *week*. We got huge. Fast. It was crazy. I was tripping; we *all* were tripping. We didn't know how to take it all in, how to deal with that success.

Sometimes we dealt with it by fighting. For once, Rebekah and I were fine, but in the band, things started to break down a bit. The pressure was intense—everyone in the media and in the industry had their eyes on us, and it was almost too much to bear. It was around then that Jonathan hit some very dark times, at least in part because he was the front man and felt the pressure the most. He started drinking a lot of Jack Daniels, which had a very negative effect on him and forced him into these phases when he'd just cry and cry, all night long. Jonathan had a bodyguard, named Loc, who basically put him on suicide watch because he would talk incessantly about killing himself. In addition to his drinking, he was struggling with anxiety, and so he saw a lot of doctors to try and treat this problem. Unfortunately, none of them really helped him, but one day he found his miracle drug: Prozac. He started taking it, and he's been sober ever since. Seeing him calm down really helped the rest of us get over the anxiety of being famous, and when it came time to record album number four, we were all pretty well adjusted to the fame.

While the fame was something that I'd always wanted, this was all much bigger than I had ever dreamed. It was fun, but it wasn't what I imagined it would be. I don't think that it was what any of us imagined it would be. When I used to dream about the fame and the rock star life, I always pictured myself being extremely happy. I pictured myself having fun all the time and loving life. I never saw myself as an out-of-control alcoholic and drug addict. I never imagined one of my band members would become suicidal. I never thought the pressure would be so serious that everyone in the band would fight all the time. And I certainly didn't think that I would have a wife and a daughter who would be sitting at home without me, missing me for months at a time while I was also missing them. Just about the only thing that went as I envisioned it was the satisfaction of making music, the satisfaction of having fans who loved the music that we created and loved to see us play live. It was an amazing experience, and on some days it was enough to make it all worth it. But in the end, all of the other dramas involved were even killing that excitement for me.

By then, the Korn shows were getting even more out of hand. We were playing all these huge shows because *Follow the Leader* had become so big. And because of *that*, the backstage partying was getting huge, too. I wasn't comfortable bringing Rebekah and Jennea on the road with us—there was just too much partying going on—so I had to go it alone. Now that I had started my family, I also had a plan in the back of my mind: I was going to stay in Korn and do this touring stuff for a few more years until I had enough money, then I would retire and be home with my family for the rest of my life. I even went so far as to promise Rebekah that the touring would end one day. But until then, I'd just have to stick it out.

And party.

Poor me.

Everyone in Korn was married now, and we had a rule within the band that wives could only stay out on the road for three days at a time. We would try to time our wives' visits to happen at the same time, telling them that it would be more fun if another wife was on the road with them. But really, we just wanted them to come and go so they wouldn't take up our party time.

The Korn road crew did a great job setting up our shows in each new city, but they also had another job: handing out after-show passes to any fine girls they found in the crowd. They would just go up to girls and ask them if they wanted to party with the band after the show, and most of them would say, "Yes, of course!" Unless they had a boyfriend. Sometimes those girls would ask if they could bring their boyfriend backstage, and the answer to that was always "No, the band only wants girls at the party." Some girls would leave their boyfriends right then and there. (We had a problem with underage girls backstage at first, but we started carding them—we didn't want to get sued.) After the show, our security guard would form a big line with all the girls, then check with us to make sure we were ready for them. Once we gave them the okay, the party would begin.

Despite the clichés about sex on the road, I just wasn't into this part of the rock star life. It wasn't what I'd signed up for. My family meant more to me than those girls, and also, I was never a convincing liar when it came to cheating. I just wanted to hang out on the road and play music with my friends—I wasn't into sleeping with a bunch of chicks to put notches in my belt.

A couple of the guys would get on my case a lot about not taking advantage of all these girls, but I'd just tell them I didn't care about missing out on the opportunities. Still, it bummed me out when they made fun of me. I started to feel like I was weird or something for not having sex with all these willing, anonymous women, like I wasn't a real man. Even though I didn't participate (mostly), I did see a lot of crazy stuff backstage. It was everywhere. There were always strippers backstage dancing for anyone who wanted a lap dance, and at the time that didn't seem like cheating to me, so I would join in.

Our roadies had their own bus, called the P-One Bus. Those guys partied like they were the real rock stars. They partied *hard* every single night. There were twelve dudes sleeping on that bus (which left it with a jacked-up odor), but still every night there were naked women running around on the P-One Bus. They were out of control. The P-One Bus was also the place to go if anyone wanted drugs. It seemed like those guys knew every drug dealer in every city we went to, and they were always ready to hand some stuff out. A couple of them actually wound up getting fired from our tours because of their drug use.

With all of this partying, all this drinking, and all these drugs, it was supposed to be this big fun time. We were playing bigger shows than ever for thousands of fans who dug our sound and even had our songs memorized. This wasn't like the tours when we were starting out—now we were the headliners, and people were there because of *us*. Sometimes the bands that opened for us would get booed by our fans the same way we got booed by Megadeth fans. Every night the crowd seemed to get bigger—more out of control. It was beyond anything that we'd ever thought of, and it would only continue to grow.

Although all this big stuff was happening, I was starting to get a little depressed because deep down inside, all I really wanted was to be at home with my family. Except for when we were on stage, I didn't like being on the road that much then. Besides performing, everything else I could easily give up. Despite my sadness, I never let on to the rest of the band that I was unhappy because I always covered it up with heavy partying. I was always trying to make people laugh by acting funny and doing stupid stuff—all while being wasted. That's how I've always been, I guess—getting drunk and acting like a clown was really the only way I knew how to be.

After the Family Values Tour ended, things calmed down some for us. Over the course of the tour, we'd adjusted to the idea of being famous and overcome much of our anxiety surrounding our success, but still, there were some divisions between members that remained, and these emerged when we went into the studio to record our fourth album, *Issues*. At the time, it seemed like David was getting pretty distant. He didn't seem to be all that interested in putting time into the songwriting, and it bugged all of us, especially Jonathan and Fieldy. David, in turn, was getting sick of them—he and Fieldy had never really gotten along that well, ever since the LAPD days. (Munky and I were always the neutral ones in the band—we tried not to take sides.)

But David wasn't the only problem. There were also issues with Fieldy. I mean, he had been my best friend for years, but even *I* was getting sick of him. With every album that passed, his attitude seemed to get worse and worse. He loved hip-hop, and so he was really trying to live this big rapper lifestyle, but it was giving him a huge ego. By the time we got around to recording *Issues*, we were all making fun of him behind his back, calling him a wannabe rapper and stuff like that. Why behind his back? Because we were afraid to say something to his face. No one ever wanted to get in an argument with Fieldy because he was just brutal when he argued. He would go for the jugular and say the most hurtful things he could, just to win the argument. (For the record, I've heard Fieldy has worked out his issues and is a really cool guy nowadays.)

I guess we were all tired of each other, the way any group of five people would be if they spent years together. We were a hard-working band; we spent a lot of time touring, recording, doing interviews, and making videos. We were just together a lot, and it was taking its toll on us. We had this joke that we always said while we were touring. We called every day Ground Hog Day because it was just like that Bill Murray movie. In the movie, when Bill Murray's character wakes up every day, it's the same day repeating itself over and over again. That was how it started to feel for most of us out on the road after a while: every day we woke up late in the afternoon, ate dinner, played the show, then partied until the wee hours of the morning. The next day we just repeated it.

Through all this, the shows were the only things that remained exciting to me, and after the shows were over, the rest of the day was inevitably a drag. If we could have chilled on the partying a little bit, we would have found lots of other things to do in the different cities we stayed in. But we were in a rut, and partying till dawn and sleeping all day was all anyone seemed interested in doing. As the months passed by, that routine got older and older. Not to mention the fact that, with all of us living together all the time, it was almost like we were married and we never had enough space.

So when I finally had some time to get away from those guys and head home before we started writing and recording *Issues*, it made me happy. Whenever I got home from a tour, I would be so excited and glad to be back, where things weren't always so crazy. I just knew that this new family way of living was going to work out perfectly, and when we had our addictions under control, Rebekah and I *did* work out. We really were happy. We were both really goofy, so we made each other hysterical all the time, doing funny dances or making funny faces to try and make the other person laugh. She used to make up all these pet names for me, like "Bear," and then use them in front of the Korn guys to embarrass me. Just really goofy stuff.

We had some good vacations, too. When Jennea was four months old, I took her and Rebekah on tour to Australia for a week. It was awesome. We stayed at the Gold Coast and had a blast. Later on, we went to Hawaii together and did some scuba diving and snorkeling. We also took these horseback-riding trips through the mountains to these beautiful waterfalls. We were happy and in love. But whenever it seemed like things were going good, they'd always get bad again, and every time they got bad, they'd be worse than ever.

A lot of the time, we put up a big front. My parents only lived a couple of hours away, and when we would visit them, we did our best to act like everything was okay—even though I'm sure my parents could sense something was wrong. Some of the time we really were happy, but most of the time we just acted happy in front of people and then fought a lot at home. Well, *when* I was home. Because more often than not, I was out on tour.

Being on the road all the time really did take its toll on our relationship. My absence made Rebekah resent me and my career—she had to stay home with Jennea while I was off partying and drinking. I would come home just beat up from all the drinking I did on the road and promise myself I wouldn't drink while I was back. But then, I was so used to the alcohol that my body would crave it, so I would go through withdrawals and cave in. The drinking was really beginning to take its toll on me.

In addition, I was still battling with my anger issues that I had never properly dealt with. It was just like my relationship with Shannon. When I was away from Rebekah, I would think about how much I missed her and loved her, but when I was with her, she would get on my nerves. Little things that she would say or do would set me off just like when I was a kid.

On top of that, Jennea would act strangely around me. When she was around two years old, I would come home and she would look at me weird, then go to Rebekah. Then after about an hour, she would finally come sit in my lap. She barely even knew me—it broke my heart.

And Korn never stopped touring—just touring and touring and touring. The three-days-at-a-time pact got in the way of Rebekah and Jennea coming on the road, and that made her resent the fact that she couldn't come out and live with me.

"Why can't I come with you?" Rebekah pleaded.

"You can't," I said. "It's not just *my* band. These guys have a say, too."

Then she asked me a very good question: "Why can't you just stand up to those guys, and be a fucking man and tell them that you're taking your family with you?"

I think I just told her to shut up, but the truth was I was afraid to have a confrontation with the rest of those guys—especially Fieldy. Not to mention the fact that I didn't see how it could work considering that we only had one band bus at the time.

It was hard. I wanted to be home more for my family, but I just couldn't. Music was my dream, but it was also my career; it was how I supported my family.

Rebekah would call me while I was on the road, just freaking out, asking when I was coming home, or why she couldn't be there with me. The whole thing made me think about getting my own tour bus and taking her and Jennea out on the road with me full time, but I was too cheap to actually go through with it.

Things started getting bad when Jennea was a toddler. I wouldn't hear from Rebekah for a little while, so I would call home: some days she'd be good, some days she'd be gone. I remember screaming on the answering machine, "Pick up the phone! Where the fuck are you?" She would be gone for days; I didn't know what she was doing, or where Jennea was. I don't know why—since we had done so many drugs together, and since she was a partier, and since she'd had so many incidents that looked suspicious—I expected her to be the perfect wife at home raising our daughter. I mean, I wasn't some sucker or sap—well, maybe I was, because I knew what was going on—but I chose to believe otherwise, because I loved her and wanted to make it work. Sometimes, when you love someone, you believe the best of them, in spite of the evidence, just because you love them. That was me.

And Rebekah was really worth loving. Even today, I still love her, though in a much different way. I've had to get through a lot of stuff in my own heart about her, and how dysfunctional she was, and how dysfunctional I was, but when we were both sober, we were great together. That's something I'll never forget.

When I would finally get ahold of her after she'd been missing for a few days, she would say, "Oh, I didn't hear the phone," and stuff like that. There was always an excuse—just as there had been before we were married. I just knew she was using drugs again, so I had to come up with another plan to rescue my family.

Around that time, Korn got the biggest check we had ever gotten, for twenty-five million bucks. We all totally flipped out over that amount, and I decided to impress Rebekah with my share of the money and move us back to Huntington Beach. She just didn't seem happy, and I thought if I could get her out of Redondo, she'd get off drugs.

I told her, "What if I buy you a nice house right next to the horse stables? I'll buy you a horse, and a house with a pool. You'll be close to the beach and everything."

I thought I could buy her happiness. So did she, actually. She got really excited about the idea, and we moved down there. I bought her a white house in this perfect little June Cleaver neighborhood. We were living the good life.

It was cool for a while, until we got bored one night, found an old friend, and started dibble-dabbling in drugs. We didn't go off the deep end, just a little bit of meth here and there. Sometimes we would even do speed when Jennea was there with us, but we always made an effort to make sure that she was asleep. We'd put her to bed, do some speed, try and sober up by the morning, and then be tired during the day. For whatever reason, we couldn't keep away from those drugs for very long. I expected Rebekah only to do drugs with me once or twice while I was home, and then stop doing it whenever I left. I don't know why I thought she could just stop. I mean, we moved *out* of Huntington to get away from drugs the first time, then moved *back* to Huntington to get away from drugs again. My addiction had totally blinded me to this pattern of destruction that just kept repeating itself.

Whenever I left for the road, I stopped doing drugs, but she kept going. Although she had done drugs most of her childhood, from, like, age fourteen on, I still felt responsible for her being hooked. A lot of the time, I was the one who brought the drugs into our home—I was the man of the house, and I should've been the best I could've been at being a dad and a husband. But I didn't have any self-control, so I had left myself open for anything.

Not long after Rebekah and I started doing speed again, Korn was booked for the biggest show of our career, a little thing called Woodstock 1999. Rebekah and I left Jennea with my parents for the weekend and flew to the concert for some hard-core partying. First stop: a private jet we rented with some guys in Limp Bizkit, Mack 10, and Ice Cube, and all our crews. That flight was crazy. The plane had three sections: the first was the chill lounge where Jonathan and all the sober people were; the second was where all the rappers and crew were drinking Hennessy and betting money at craps (I think Mack 10 took everyone's money on that flight); the third was for all the people that just wanted to drink and do drugs.

That's where Rebekah and I hung out.

There was a little bit of cocaine going around, but everyone mostly drank and smoked weed. I remember when the cocaine ran out, some of the Korn roadie crew started snorting Tylenol PM. I told you they were nuts. Not that I wasn't.

Anyway, all of us in Korn were so nervous about playing. There were over two hundred thousand people attending that concert, not to mention the hundreds of millions watching on satellite TV. It was crazy.

To add to our nervousness, it seemed like it took forever for the show to start, and as show time approached all I could think about was how hard my heart was beating. When the lights finally went out, we started the intro to our first song, "Blind." In the intro, we each had our own part that built the song up to this crazy, heavy groove that no crowd could deny. David started with his ride symbol. The crowd roared so loudly it pierced my ears. Then Munky jumped in with his part. The crowd got even louder. Fieldy's bass part came next. More roars. After that I started the opening riff to the instrumental hook of the song—the heavy groove. By that time, Jonathan screamed his opening line that never failed to put the crowd into a frenzy: "Arrrrrre yooooouuu *readdddddyyyyyyyyyy* ?!?!?!" When he screamed those words and the heavy groove kicked in, a sea of people jumped up and down at the same time, creating a wave that spread throughout the crowd.

It was an awesome beginning to an amazing show. Afterwards, we all hugged each other—even David and Fieldy. And then came the after-party. Woodstock had rented out this hotel for all the bands, and there was a party on every floor. Rebekah and I took some ecstasy and did a bunch of cocaine that night. We stayed up all night and fought most of the time. The next day, we partied more on the plane until we landed and got into a limo that was waiting for us. Still a little too high from the cocaine, we started drinking in the limo on the way home to level us out before we saw my parents and Jennea.

It was about 5 PM, and we were pretty drunk when we got home, so Rebekah decided she should sober up by diving in the pool. And that's what she did. Shirt, pants, shoes, and everything. She walked right past my parents, said a quick hello, and then dove in. When she came up out of the water, she had a bump on her head from hitting the bottom of the pool. I was trying to talk to my parents without slurring, but that was pretty much impossible. They were definitely looking at us funny, but after a little while they left.

When my parents left, around 8 PM, we put Jennea to bed. The house got so quiet and we were so drunk and tired that it only made sense for us to go to bed. But we didn't. We started arguing about something stupid (I don't even remember what), and the argument quickly escalated into screaming. Rebekah got right into my face and wouldn't stop yelling. She charged me pretty hard, so I lost control and punched her in the face. Blood started pouring out of her nose, down her face and neck.

I was very shocked at what I had done. I felt so horrible.

I thought that would stop the screaming, but she got even angrier, and it made the situation much worse. After seeing all the blood, I told her I was so sorry and that I wasn't gonna fight with her any longer. But she ended up beating me up for a while. I just laid on the floor with my face in the carpet taking punches from her. Finally, after about twenty minutes, she collapsed on the floor and passed out. I remember sitting on the floor, shaking and crying while my wife laid next to me all bloody and passed out. It was definitely a gutter moment, me sitting there thinking, *Why is my life so messed up? I have everything I need in life to be happy.* That weekend was supposed to be the best time of my life, but it turned into one of the worst.

At that point, things weren't looking too good for me and Rebekah, but there was one last moment of hope before all hell broke loose in our marriage. Rebekah ran into one of her old hard-core buddies who went by the name of "Scottish." Scottish used to slam a lot of heroin back in the day, but now he had cleaned up and gotten married. He had made a huge turnaround, and when Rebekah ran into him, it really inspired her.

Because of that run-in, she convinced me that we could do the same thing. We got really excited talking and dreaming of our future together, of being totally clean for good. Rebekah talked to Scottish a few times on the phone, and he always injected a lot of positive energy and life into her. Then one day, Rebekah got a call from Scottish's wife. He had relapsed. And overdosed.

And died.

Rebekah was crushed, and just like that, every ounce of hope she'd built up went down the toilet.

Shortly after Scottish's overdose, it was once again time for me to go on tour—this time with Metallica and Kid Rock, and that was when Rebekah's drug habit progressed from bad to worse. While I was on that tour, she started partying nonstop. One day on the tour, I got a call from a friend telling me about some crazy parties going on at my house. Noise. Crazy skinhead dudes. Throwing, breaking stuff. I called my house, but Rebekah wouldn't answer, or someone else would answer, say she wasn't there, and then hang up on me. The worst part was that I didn't know where Jennea was during all this partying. I was helpless. It was a complete nightmare.

I had heard that she was hanging out with this one particular guy at the time. He was a skinhead and a second-strike felon, and when I asked her about him, she would always tell me, "Yeah, he's an old friend from the old days. He's like my brother. I'm trying to help him out." Yes, it was true—he was an old friend from the old days, just like Scottish had been. But he wasn't clean, and I knew he wasn't just a friend, either.

I bought her excuses for awhile, just as I always had, but then I got a call from a friend of mine who happened to work in a pawn shop. He told me some skinhead guy had gone in there trying to sell a solid gold necklace medallion that said "Korn" on it. I recognized that medallion— a record executive had a few made up and had given one as a personal gift to every guy in Korn. And now some skinhead was trying to get two hundred bucks for it in a pawn shop.

I freaked out and called Rebekah. "What's going on?" I was expecting her to give me more excuses about needing money to help out a friend or something like that. What she said was the last thing I expected to hear:

"I'm leaving you."

I lost it. "What do you mean you're *leaving* me?"

"I'm fucking leaving you!" she said, screaming. "I'm going to divorce you and take half your money!"

I was totally shocked. This couldn't be happening. My worst fear was coming true. I was determined not to let her go. I said, "I'm sorry, Rebekah. Look, we can work out whatever we need to work out. I'll get my own tour bus and take you and Jennea on tour with me wherever I go."

"No," she said. "I'm leaving you."

It was too late.

And I lost all control. That was one of the worst days of my life. I pleaded with her on the phone not to leave me, but it didn't do me any good. I asked her if she had been screwing around with that guy, but she denied it. You know, that's what got to me the most—that she wouldn't admit it. In the face of all the evidence, all the stories, all the incidents, she wouldn't admit it.

My whole world was falling apart, and it drove me crazy. It drove me back to cocaine, actually. I started doing a lot of coke, just as a way of dealing with the pain of Rebekah leaving me. I was so shocked and angry. I didn't know how to cope, so I coped the best way available and the only way I really knew: drugs.

I tried calling Rebekah a couple of times to talk her out of it, but she wouldn't even answer my calls. Finally, I got ahold of her a few days before a scheduled three-day break in our current tour. I let her know I was going to fly home during the break to see her and Jennea. I figured I had one last chance to grab both my girls and save them from the drug-induced madness happening in our home. I hoped with everything in me that I could talk some sense into Rebekah. A couple of days before my break, I called home again, but instead of getting Rebekah, I heard Jennea's babysitter on the other end of the line. She told me that Rebekah had hired her to watch Jennea for a few days. Why? Because Rebekah had split for Oregon, where her mother lived (in a house we'd bought for her). Rebekah knew I was going to try to talk her out of leaving me, so, instead of sticking around to listen, she took off. I guess she left Jennea there because she knew I missed her and needed to see her.

When I got home and spoke to the babysitter, I was able to piece together Rebekah's plan, which went something like this: Give Jennea to the babysitter, then get out of town to avoid seeing me. While she was gone, she figured that the babysitter would hand Jennea over to me, and I would spend my three days with Jennea. Once it was time for me to go back on tour, I would give Jennea back to the babysitter at which point Rebekah would return from Oregon and pick up where she left off.

It did not take long for Rebekah's plan to change. Just a few hours after I talked to the babysitter, my mother-in-law called me from Oregon. She said Rebekah had just arrived, but that she'd brought a bunch of partying skinheads with her, and now they were terrorizing the place. There was fighting—bare-knuckle fighting—going on upstairs in that

Oregon house. I guess they were having skinhead brawls up there or something. There was blood on the carpet, kids doing drugs, all kinds of crazy stuff going on.

My mother-in-law said she felt like she was in a horror movie, so she frantically told me I had to go to Huntington, get Jennea, and take her out on the road with me. Apparently, Rebekah was going to be heading back to our house in Huntington Beach soon, and my mother-in-law was terrified for Jennea to be around all that skinhead madness. The drugs had turned Rebekah into a monster, and all these people she was hanging out with were making her worse.

After that phone call, I knew that her mother was absolutely right: I would have to take Jennea on the road with me full-time from there on out. I mean, if Rebekah was doing all that stuff in Oregon, then she had to be acting the same way at home.

In retrospect, everything about this time was really traumatizing. Once I had that conversation with my mother-in-law, I became so anxious to get home. While I was freaked out because Rebekah had left me and I was grieving her loss as though she had died, I had no time to grieve. It was time for me to be a father, and I knew what I had to do.

As soon as I could, I flew home, picked up Jennea, hired a nanny, and went back out on the road with her. In just a couple of days, I had become a rock star single dad, but being around Jennea took away a lot of my pain about Rebekah. Of course, I didn't have much time to worry about myself—I was too worried about Jennea losing her mother to care about my own loss. All I focused on was making sure my baby was okay. It was just the two of us now.

SIX

I FALL TO PIECES . . .

I surprised myself at how well I held together for the rest of that tour. It was so painful to see Jennea and know that her mother was not there for her anymore. But while I missed Rebekah too, I felt better just looking at this beautiful, smiling, little girl every day. Everyone else loved her, too. All the guys in the band and on the road crew would take turns hanging out with her—she was very popular. Even our big security guards would hang out with her and take her for stroller rides. She was a huge hit.

Despite all of the insanity, I still had this hope that Rebekah and I could work things out. A tiny part of me really wanted to believe that this dude she had left me for was *really* just a friend. I thought that if she could just see me with Jennea, she would realize what she had done and come back for good. I couldn't admit to myself that our relationship was over.

Every now and then, Rebekah would call to tell me that she needed money. During one of those phone calls, she admitted to me for the first time that her skinhead "friend" was actually her boyfriend. I had known the truth already, but still it sucked to hear it and it really hurt.

And then my pride kicked in: *How can I let this guy take my wife away from me? How can I let this woman make me look like a peon in front of every-one? Don't they know who I am? I'm a rich and famous rock star! I have real gangsters working for me! All I have to do is say the word, and I can have my revenge.* It was a power trip to me, a way of getting back, of proving that they couldn't do this to me. But in the end, these fantasies didn't do anything to make me feel better and they didn't bring Rebekah back to me.

While I was on tour with Jennea, Rebekah went back to Hunting-ton Beach from Oregon and stayed at our house again, since I wasn't there. Not surprisingly, she brought all of her crazy, skinhead friends back with her. I didn't want those guys living in my house, so I decided to call on one of my Bako friends who happened to live in Huntington Beach, a guy I just called "D." Since D was known in Bako for being one of the toughest guys in town, I asked him if he could go over to my house and kick everyone out. He agreed. Just to be fair, I called Rebekah and left a message, warning her that I was sending someone over to change the locks and that she'd better be gone.

D didn't know what to expect, so he stopped by a friend's house on the way over to borrow a gun, just in case. Fortunately, instead of Re-bekah and all her *Fight Club* skinhead friends, he only found that seven-teen-year-old babysitter Rebekah had hired. She was having a good old time living in my house with her new boyfriend. He booted them out and got the locks changed.

Rebekah talked a lot about taking my money in the divorce, and naturally I was scared at first that she could do it. We would go back and forth on the phone, and she would insist that I give her half of everything, and then I would tell her I would kill her before that would ever happen. In the end, I offered her a specific, one-time settlement, and she took it. She signed the papers, and we were officially divorced. It was for real.

But there was one thing left to do: figure out who got custody of Jennea. We both wanted full custody, and Rebekah fought with me on the phone about that all the time. I really did want her to be able to hang out with Jennea, because I knew my daughter needed a mom as much as she needed a dad, but Rebekah was hooked up with this crazy guy and acting like a monster. I didn't want Jennea anywhere near her. Eventually, we set a court date for our custody hearing that would take place six months later, and when Rebekah didn't show up, I got full custody.

Soon after D cleared out my house and had the locks changed, I finished the tour and came home with Jennea. The band had planned a huge break after that tour, so I had some time to process all the craziness that had been going on in my life lately. While having the down time should have been great, I became incredibly depressed just being in that house that I bought for Rebekah. Rebekah's stuff was there, but Rebekah wasn't. It was like when Shannon left me, all over again. She'd been there, and now she wasn't. I felt like Rebekah died.

It depressed me so much that, a couple of nights after I got home, I decided to put Jennea to bed early so I could get drunk by myself. When she went to sleep, I started in on the beer. I was also a heavy smoker at the time, but I never smoked inside the house, so I kept going in and out of the house to have a cigarette, hanging out in this lounge chair by the pool that I always sat in. After I'd gotten good and wasted, and smoked my last cigarette, I wandered back into the house and passed out on the couch. A couple of hours later, I woke up and figured I should go check on Jennea, so I went into her room—and freaked.

She wasn't there.

I panicked. I started screaming her name at the top of my lungs and turning the place upside-down. I couldn't find her anywhere. Somehow, I wound up back at the couch where I had passed out, and I noticed that I had left the back door open, the door that led to the backyard.

To the pool.

My mind immediately jumped to the worst possible scenario: Jennea had wandered into the pool, and I was going to find her out there, drowned. I mean, what were the odds? I couldn't find my baby anywhere in the house, the back door was open—it didn't take a genius to figure out she was outside somewhere. When I started to walk outside, I was so afraid of what I was going to find, but as I approached the pool, my heart flooded with relief. Curled up in that lounge chair I always sat in was my little girl, fast asleep. I guess she had woken up in the middle of the night and wandered out there, figuring that's where she could find me.

I picked her up and held her for a long, long time. I was so thankful she was still alive. I vowed right then and there to clean myself up so I could be the dad she deserved. But even the thought of my own daughter almost drowning couldn't keep me clean for very long.

Shortly after this happened, D and I started hanging out more, and we became really good friends. D had a wife and two kids, and it was nice to hang out with another family, where Jennea could have sort of a motherly influence. D was a great support for me, and we became inseparable through all my divorce and custody problems.

Also, D had just gotten his real estate license, and so after talking about things, we decided to start a real estate business to make some big cash, which was exciting since D knew what he was doing, and it gave me something to focus on while I was off the road.

D also knew that I needed help with Jennea, so he and his wife really welcomed us into their family. They assisted me with a lot of the day-to-day parenting stuff like potty training Jennea. I eventually ended up hiring D's wife as a full-time nanny for the next few years and Jennea stayed with them every time I had to go on tour. At the same time, D and I were having a blast making money in real estate and generally hanging out. I became closer to them than I was to my own family. It really helped me get over the pain of losing Rebekah; for the first time in a while, I felt like hope was a part of my life.

Things were on a good road, but it didn't take long for them to get bumpy again. D and I were great drinkers. We had a lot of fun drinking together, but eventually we started getting into something a little more serious. Drugs. Because I had seen what speed did to Rebekah, I had sworn it off for good by then, but I figured cocaine would be all right. I could still function on coke—it didn't jack me up like speed did, so D and I started doing it together.

But I tired of coke pretty quickly too. I realized that I was just falling back into my old habits, and I didn't want to do that. I wanted to shake my drug addiction, and so, before the cocaine use got way out of hand, D and I got rid of it. I switched to Xanax and Vicodin, which to me didn't seem like real drugs because everyone took pills, and I could get them from doctors. I had all kinds of friends who were doctors and could get me these drugs on the road. Legally. I would call all of them, too, so I could stock up on pills.

I would have three hundred pills going of each brand at a time. We had doctors coming to our shows all the time—one of them would bring us nitrous tanks, and we would inhale balloons all night, and then he would write us prescriptions for whatever we wanted. It made me feel like a kid in a candy store. I remember one surgeon came to our show with a lot of drugs. He would tell us the coke and ecstasy that he had was made from his pharmacist friend and that it was the best you could get. He would party with us until 6:00 AM and then complain that he had to go work in the emergency room at 9:00 to go do surgery on people.

Crazy, crazy stuff, man.

Anyway, after D and I had been hanging out for a while, we decided to move our families out of Huntington Beach and back to Bakersfield. I felt it was the perfect place to start my life all over. With my parents and brother (and his family) there, it was a great opportunity for Jennea to be around her blood family more often. It was also a great opportunity for me and D to be sober together, and when we hit Bako, we were clean and sober. Of course, I had tried moving away from drugs before, and it had never worked—I don't know why I was convinced it would work this time.

As I was preparing for the move back to Bako, the big break from Korn was coming to a close, and we were preparing to start writing our fifth album, *Untouchables*. We decided for this album that we needed a change of scenery as a band, that we needed to get away from everything—our families and all—and concentrate on writing music. A couple of the guys were also going through divorces at that time, so it was good for all of us to get out of Dodge. (Eventually, we all ended up getting divorced, by the way. Just as we watched each other start our families, we watched each other lose them. Our rock 'n' roll lifestyle was just too crazy for most people to stick around us for too long.)

Together we settled on Arizona as a destination. To make things easier for me, I left my little girl with D and his family, which undoubtedly was a smart move given the craziness that was ahead. We wound up renting these four huge houses in Scottsdale, Arizona, moving in our equipment, and heading out there to get to work. It was a great idea, but it had just one problem: it turned into some of the most intense partying

I'd ever seen Korn do. Fortunately, I was sober, and so was Jonathan. The other three band members—and our crew—were not. They went at it *hard*.

The four house setup was convenient for the different lifestyles that were going on. Munky and I shared a house with the crew, and that's where we did most of the songwriting. There was a studio set up in the basement for recording demos, and since I was trying to be sober, this was usually the sober house. On the other hand, David had a house to himself, which quickly became one of the major party houses. Jonathan also had a house to himself where there was yet another studio, so I'd go over there at night to do some additional writing with him. I wanted to do what I could to stay sober. Finally, Fieldy had the last house, and it was the craziest. He even had a stripper's pole installed, and just generally had wild parties every night.

So, there you go. It was so hard to be sober for the three months I was out there—there was just so much partying going on, and I have to admit that, when we first got to Arizona, I found myself at Fieldy's house quite a bit. But mostly I remained faithful to the deal D and I had made and wound up hanging by myself at my house. I just didn't really want to be around anyone else in the band—it wasn't fun being around drunks when *I* wasn't drunk.

After we wrote *Untouchables*, we headed to L.A. to record, and when the album was done, it was time to hit the road yet again. By that point, we were all pretty tired of each other's personalities, so we each got our own tour buses. Five tour buses, on the road together. We hardly made any money on that tour because of all the money we spent getting from show to show, but it was worth it—we simply couldn't live with each other anymore.

I wasn't on the road very long before I started falling into my same old tricks. Since I left the responsibility of raising Jennea on D's wife, I dove right back into drinking, drugs, partying. You know the drill—except this time, I decided I wanted to become like the other guys and try to hook up with a different girl every night. I mean, I was single now. What was stopping me? Maybe *that's* what I had been missing the whole time—maybe *that's* what I needed to feel satisfied.

It didn't last long, though. I had my security guard Joshua looking for girls for me every night and when he found them, it would always end up in a disaster. One night after I slept with this pretty Spanish girl, it came time for the tour bus to leave and I told her she had to get off the bus. She ended up smacking me in the face and screaming at me that she wasn't a "horror." Another time, I met this other girl who begged me to choke her in the back of my tour bus because it turned her on. After a few episodes like those, I couldn't do it anymore; it just wasn't me. No, my thing was drugs, and that's precisely what I did for most of the *Untouchables* tour.

Back in Bako, in between tours, I met a new friend, a cool guy who had a lot in common with me, including a past addiction to meth. We wound up talking a lot about our past with speed, and over time we talked so much that we both started wanting it. We ended up getting some, and though I had sworn to myself and to D that I would never do it again, I decided that it wouldn't hurt to do it once. After that, I decided that it wouldn't hurt to do it once in a while.

I didn't want to tell D about it, though, because, well, I knew he would kill me if he found out. So I kept it to myself, doing speed every now and then without telling anyone. I didn't think it would turn me into a monster, like it had done with Rebekah, and I was totally sure I could keep it under control. But after I had done it a few times, I started getting a little moody in between uses, and D's wife began to suspect

something. She could tell I was up to no good, and she and I started getting into these huge arguments because of it.

Things were made all the more stressful between us because she
was the one who took care of Jennea (and her own two kids) when I
would go on the road. I just wasn't myself, and she knew it. I was giving
her so much attitude about the way she was taking care of my kid that
one day she got fed up with it and told me she couldn't watch Jennea
anymore. The two of them were close, but she couldn't take my attitude
for one more day. That sent me over the edge. In my crazy mind, all I
saw was another motherly woman walking out of Jennea's life, and it
both depressed me and made me kind of hate her for it.

Now that I see things clearly, I can see that I pushed her out of our
lives with my addiction, but at the time, I was convinced that it was all
her fault. The speed gave me a distorted view of life, so I started calling
D's wife and saying mean things to her. I would call her names, or say
crazy stuff. Of course, D couldn't stand for that, so we had a big falling-
out, and we all stopped talking to each other.

After all that stuff happened, I realized I had a choice to make: my
music career or my daughter. I couldn't have both. And since they were
both a huge part of my life, it didn't matter which one I picked—it was
going to kill me to be without either of them. Speed became my escape,
a way to avoid making the choice, a way to put it off a little longer.
Rather than trying to get myself cleaned up and taking the responsibility
for raising my daughter, I asked my parents to take care of Jennea while
I went on tour and shoved more alcohol and drugs into my body. My life
was a big, horrible mess. My career was great, but my personal life was
nothing but bad news. One horrible thing after another kept happening,
and I couldn't understand why.

I was so depressed about the whole situation—I had all this money, all this fame, but I was really missing out on all the good stuff in life. My relationships with my friends were horrible. People kept bailing on me and Jennea. I wasn't raising my daughter right. I felt like I had to quit my band, and I couldn't.

So I turned to drugs as hard as I could. Speed. Coke. Pills. Alcohol. Every day.

I knew I had to shake the drugs, but I just couldn't. For one thing, I was too addicted—part of me didn't want to quit. For another, they were everywhere. No matter where I went, I would find them. If I was at home, I would run into some friends who were users. If I was on tour, I couldn't go anywhere without seeing a pile of coke. I had nowhere to run.

The first tour I did in the middle of this drug-soaked depression was Ozzfest, during a beautiful summer that I paid absolutely no attention to. Though we played with a ton of great bands that summer, I don't think I saw a single one of them—not even Ozzy. Instead, I just sat in the back room of my tour bus, alone, every night. I had a security guard/friend named Joshua living in the front part of my bus, and he would always try and get me to do fun things, but I never wanted to leave my room. Most everyone in the band and crew came to my bus at one time or another to make an attempt to get me to come and hang out with them, but I always told them that I wanted to be alone.

Sometimes I heard Ozzy performing those same songs I listened to when I was a kid, but I never went to watch him. That enthusiasm from Korn's early days was gone. I just sat there in so much dark depression and asked myself deep questions. *How did I get here? Why can't I enjoy this life? Isn't being a rock star supposed to be fun? Why is my life such a nightmare? Why do bad things keep happening to me?* It felt like I was under a curse, honestly. I was stuck. And it didn't look like I was ever going to get out.

The drugs really started to get in the way of my guitar playing, too. I looked terrible. I started having thoughts about how it would be a relief if I would OD in my tour bus or in a hotel room. When you first do speed, you feel bigger than you really are. It makes you concentrate really hard, really get fixed on something. If your mind is set on something good (music, sex), then everything will feel so much better than normal. But if you're thinking about negative things (loneliness, depression), the drug causes such darkness in your mind, that everything seems much worse than it really is. It's just the way the drug works.

I loved that "good" feeling, but I became a slave to it. I wanted to quit so bad—I had been promising myself for months that I would quit after this tour or that tour or this month or that month, but I never could shake it. I was addicted physically *and* mentally. With the depression and disillusionment that the drug gave me, I had convinced myself that I might not ever be able to quit—and if I quit the band, I would never be able to be a normal, happy person. And that's why I started thinking about death. It seemed like it might be a good escape for me. In my darkest moments it just felt like it was the only way out and the easiest, since by that time I was convinced that death meant I would just turn into dust and sleep forever.

Those dark thoughts wouldn't last forever though. I would eventually snap out of it, get my mind off of me, and think about Jennea. I would wonder how she felt when she thought about her mom and dad not being around like the other kids at school. I would think about how unloved and rejected she must've felt sometimes, but for some reason I kept on doing drugs to avoid facing my responsibilities as a father.

I spent day by day, week by week, and month by month using meth. I didn't miss one day because I couldn't get out of bed without it. Whether I was on tour or at home with Jennea, I always had speed in my system.

Sometime in the beginning of 2003, Korn was getting ready to go on a world tour, and instead of being excited, my first priority was packing. I spent two days packing my stuff so I could get my drugs nice and hidden, stashed away where no one could find them. This tour went all over the world: China, Japan, all over Europe, Australia, and New Zealand. And everywhere the tour took me, I made sure to bring along enough speed to last, hiding it in my suitcase inside containers of deodorant, or in my clothes, or in vitamin capsules. We rolled through a country in Asia where the penalty for drug trafficking—even if you had a single joint in your suitcase—was death, and I didn't care, because part of me wanted to be dead. And besides, I didn't know how to get speed on the road in another country, so I had to make sure I had my stash with me.

While you'd think that an addiction as bad as mine would be hard to hide, I did a really good job of keeping it from my bandmates. Mainly, I just stayed away from them until I had to do something, and then I drank a few beers or took a Xanax (or Valium or Vicodin) to calm myself down so I wouldn't look so tweaked out. Of course, they knew something was wrong. They noticed how skinny I was getting, but they thought I was just on pills (which I was), and somehow that was okay.

Remember, speed is a dirty drug—pills are something that you can get from a doctor. In our band, taking pills was like eating lunch or smoking weed; it was something that everyone did. Almost everyone else on tour was addicted to something (except Jonathan—unless you count Big Macs), but they weren't so addicted that they hid their drugs

This was taken when I was about five. Even then I had a habit of making a mess.

Growing up was hard for a lot of reasons, but especially when I got picked on. Here you can start to see where the name "Head" came from.

This was the closest that I came to Chevron-approved hair.

Soccer ball head. This is when I shaved my hair off just before the Sick of It All tour.

Jennea, shortly after she was born. She brought the most amazing light into my life and it's been there ever since.

When "Freak on a Leash" hit in 1999, we realized that things had gotten pretty big. That year we appeared at the MTV Video Music Awards and we didn't leave empty-handed. We took home two awards for our "Freak on a Leash" video.

Amid all the craziness, Rebekah, Jennea, and I took some pretty awesome vacations. This picture was taken at the Gold Coast during Korn's tour in Australia. I was nervous bringing Jennea this close to the tigers, but they were gentle.

When I wasn't touring, I tried to be there for Jennea, and do more normal things with her, like here when we posed for pictures together. In the end though, the drugs and my lifestyle made forming a close bond with her really hard.

Even when things were at their worst, it always felt good to get up on stage and play for our fans.

One year we worked with MTV so that a fan could direct the video for our song "Alone I Break." This photo was taken during the filming of that contest.

This was me at my worst in 2004. It was taken in between songs at one of our shows, when my body was filled with meth, pills, beer, and peanut butter and jelly sandwiches. At that point I had almost no energy to go on with the concert—or life

Though things were sometimes rough with the band, we really knew how to put on a great show.

The day that God helped me say good-bye to meth for good was one of the best days of my life. With his help, I flushed everything down the toilet, and I've been clean ever since.

My baptism in the Jordan River was one of the most amazing experiences of my spiritual life. Traveling there and being in the same water that Jesus felt—there's nothing that can compare.

BRIAN "HEAD" WELCH
HOME FOR CHILDREN

...PPY & HOLY HOME SOCIE...
SPOND. BY GOOD NEWS INDIA.
...HOOL & ASH... (ORPHANAGE)
REGISTERED BY REGIST... ...961 AND FCRA

The trip to India and to Head Home was unbelievable. It opened my eyes to a world that I knew nothing about and completely changed my perspective on Christ's power to help people everywhere.

The members of the Loadi tribe.

This shot was taken when I reunited with Kevin. It was cool to tell him about the role that he played in my decision to follow Christ.

God and Jennea are the center of my world. Everything I do, I do for them.

and toted them into other countries. That was just me. But those guys never stopped making attempts to get me to hang out with them. That whole time I was on drugs, they always showed concern for me because deep down I'm sure they knew something was wrong.

Like Ozzfest, much of the world tour was a blur. All I did was hang out by myself and do drugs, only this time, instead of missing Ozzy, I missed out on some of the world's coolest countries. But it didn't matter to me. Nothing really mattered to me—nothing, that is, except for the drugs and my computer. When I was high on meth, I became obsessed with my computer; it became my best friend. All I did when I was high on that world tour was try to write music on my computer for hours at a time, or look at porno on the Internet.

When we finished the world tour, I went home to Jennea, but I didn't stop using. I would spend a little time with her during the day, but at night, after she was asleep, I was off to my closet to snort some lines. Sometimes, Jennea would wake up in the middle of the night and see me at my computer or whatever, totally high on speed, and ask me why I was awake. She always looked worried and would sometimes cry, like she knew something was wrong with me. I would tell her that I had just woken up, and that I was going back to bed soon, but it didn't comfort her all that much. She was worried about her dad.

I started buying tons of meth from this drug dealer I hooked up with in Bako. He would come over to my house in the middle of the night while Jennea was sleeping, and he would bring his shotgun with him, because I was just one of many stops he had that night. We sort of became prison buddies—I was stuck in my addiction, and he was stuck dealing drugs to support his family.

If you've never done meth before, one thing you have to understand is that there are different brands, and sometimes addicts get so used to one brand to where it stops working as well, so you have to switch to a different brand. Anytime my dealer got a new brand, he would call me, and I would tell him to come over so I could buy a stash. I was so addicted that I had eight brands going at once. *Eight* different brands of speed. In addition to all those pills, and all the beer. I was so afraid I would run out that I bought plenty to have on hand. I had this safe in my room that was just filled with meth. I had this one particular kind that was cut with something weird, and I was afraid to do it, but I was also afraid to throw it away. Instead, I just stuck it with the rest and kept adding to my collection.

And this whole time, I had my kid living with me—my precious, five-year-old daughter, who could only sit back and watch as her dad wasted away on drugs.

SEVEN

. . . AND GET PUT
BACK TOGETHER

Although I had done a good job of messing up almost every area of my life, the one way in which I was actually doing something right was money. In fact by 2004, I was close to being set for life. I was making a lot of cash, and I wasn't wasting it. Instead, I was back in the real estate business, not with D, but with this guy that I met named Doug. He was a regular guy from Bakersfield who had a great family and was smart and in charge of his life. He was also a church-going Christian and something of a goodie-goodie in a way that reminded me of my old childhood friend Kevin. And just like Kevin, he was always happy and upbeat, always in a good mood. He was just an all-around positive person, and I was really drawn to him.

Unlike Kevin, Doug never talked about Jesus or God with me. Our relationship was strictly business—the only way I knew that he was Christian was because someone else told me. Working together, we had a good time making real estate deals in Bako, and when we made those deals, we used Doug's broker, a guy named Eric, who also happened to be Christian and also happened to have his life together.

I really liked hanging out with these guys, mostly because they were just so positive, not to mention the fact that they were good businessmen. I trusted the decisions that they made and I felt like I could make a lot of cash in real estate by working with them. When I was thinking more positively, that became the goal that I carried in the back of my mind: get clean, get up enough nerve to quit Korn, then do real estate for the rest of my life.

Since I toured so much with Korn, I often had to do my real estate business while I was on the road. One day I was on tour and I called Eric to talk about some business. I wound up getting into a conversation with him about my life and how hard it was finding a balance between the band and my daughter. I told him how I was considering quitting the band, and he said something that really got me to thinking.

He said, "You know, Brian, no one ever says on their deathbed that they wished they would've worked more. They always wish they had spent more time with their family."

And it hit me right there.

It was suddenly clear: I thought about Jennea, and how if I quit the band to be with her, I would have no regrets. If I stayed in the band, however, there would be all kinds of regrets. The problem was that I didn't have the balls to quit Korn. It was a big step for me. We were at the height of our career. Professionally, things couldn't have been better. We were selling tons of records, playing these huge shows, going all over the place, and every time I would start thinking about quitting, the drugs would get in the way. They just kept fueling my selfishness.

I couldn't think straight about the whole thing, let alone make a decision. One day I would want to quit the band, the next day I would want

to stay. I decided to get off drugs so I could make a clear, rational, responsible decision. My plan became this: kick the drugs for now, most
likely quit the band, raise my kid, and then when she was all grown up, I
could go back to drugs later in life. I found this clinic in L.A. that special-
ized in helping actors and musicians get clean, this really incognito place
that kept everything quiet. I liked the idea of going there to get a secret
cure for my secret addiction, so I checked them out. They gave me some
meds that would help me get past the initial withdrawals, and I remember wondering how useful those meds would be. I was no stranger to
withdrawals, but I had never in my life done drugs so many days in a
row—and I didn't know how hard the comedown would really be.

I left my kid with my parents, checked myself into a hotel, and took
the meds that clinic had given me. I tried to go to sleep, but I couldn't—
all I could do was lay there and feel depressed. The depression got worse
and worse, and I started feeling like I would go insane if I didn't do a line
right then. The meds were powerless against the drug. I went home and
dove into my stash. In that instant, I gave up on quitting; it wasn't going
to work this time. I really made an attempt to quit, and when I failed, it
was very scary to me because it confirmed all of my worst fears: I was unable to escape meth.

What lifted me, at least slightly, out of my depression, was getting back
to work with the band. We hit the studio to make album number six,
Take A Look In The Mirror. Though it felt good to start working with the
band again, the recording process did little to curb my addictions. I don't
have a whole lot of memories of that time, because I used speed during
the whole period we recorded and toured for that album.

The optimism that I felt when we started recording quickly evaporated when we hit the road. I just did the same stuff. Toured with Korn on dope. Went home on dope. I wasn't doing anything with anyone. I refused interviews. I even started to hate playing live. I'd had enough of everybody and everything.

After we toured for that album, we put out a "Greatest Hits" record, and to give it a few singles for radio and MTV, we recorded a couple of cover songs. One of the songs was "Another Brick in The Wall" by Pink Floyd, and it has this really famous solo in it that I was supposed to record in the studio. I barely pulled it off because I was so high. The other cover was of that Cameo song "Word Up," and I wasn't too happy about playing that song. I disliked the video even more. They put our heads on some dogs and showed us hanging out as dogs in strip clubs. I think it was supposed to be funny, but I didn't see how. I thought it was stupid. A couple of the other guys in the band weren't too into it, either.

Anyway, as a band, I felt like we were losing our creativity. Some of the guys felt like we needed to reinvent our sound, and so we started talking about hiring out hit songwriters for our next album. It really struck me as a bad idea that I just wasn't into at all. My feeling was, I would rather have written stupid crap on our own than hire Top 40 hit songwriters. That just felt like selling out to me. It wasn't what Korn was all about.

I started to feel like the focus of the band was less on the love of music and more on making money, on putting out a marketable product. I know I used a lot of drugs then, but for some reason, when it came to making music and making money, I was usually pretty clear about what I wanted to do. These creative problems in the band just made the idea of leaving that much more appealing.

In the summer of 2004, Korn headed to Europe for a tour, and it started to look like I wasn't going to have to leave the band—it looked like we were headed for a breakup. Or at the least that we were going to lose a member or two. At the time, both Jonathan and Fieldy had girlfriends, and both women came on that tour with us. The only problem: the two girlfriends started to hate each others' guts, and they started fighting a lot. Naturally, Jonathan and Fieldy also started fighting with each other to the point where Jonathan wanted to kick Fieldy out of the band. All the fighting seemed childish to me, but, by the same token, it also seemed like it could be my way out of the band. I was disgusted with the way these guys were acting, so I asked my tour manager to get me a ticket home, but he wouldn't do it.

I was stuck. Just like with drugs, I couldn't bring myself to quit, but I wanted someone or something *else* to make the decision for me, to take me out. I was addicted to the band, and I was addicted to drugs. Both of them were sucking the life out of me, and I knew I had to quit them both. But I couldn't. Jonathan and Fieldy wound up working it out, and we made it through the tour without canceling it.

We all had road rage, really. Things were just crazy, and the craziest thing was that I was the peacemaker during those times. I really didn't want the whole band to break up; I just wanted to quit being in it, so I would try to help everyone get along. Munky also did a lot of peacemaking during that time, trying to keep everything together.

But I had my moments of temper, just like the rest of them. I was playing like crap, so I started taking it out on my guitar tech during our shows. I remember one time when I got so pissed off about my horrible playing that I took my guitar off and literally threw it at my tech. Like it was his fault that I sucked. He ducked, and it flew backstage where a bunch of people were walking by; luckily, it didn't hit anyone.

In the middle of 2004, I was just saturated with evil and depression. I was doing more speed than you can imagine. I was getting more obsessed with pornography on the Internet, turning into more of a sicko than I already was. I had hit rock bottom.

I was in the gutter.

And I was dragging my beautiful five-year-old daughter down with me. This was around the time that I caught her singing the Korn song "A.D.I.D.A.S." I was already in the gutter, but hearing that song come out of Jennea's mouth really made me feel like a piece of trash. I knew it was time for me to try and reach out for help, so I reached out to Doug and Eric a little bit. I sent them e-mails about real estate deals all the time, and in some of them I started to hint at how unhappy I was—not just with the band, but with life itself.

One morning I got an e-mail out of the blue from Eric:

Brian:

Not to get weird on you or anything, but I was reading my Bible this morning and you came to mind when I read this verse:

"Come to me, all who are weary and burdened and I will give you rest. Take my yoke upon you and learn from me, for I am gentle and humble in heart, there you will find rest for your souls. For my yoke is easy and my burden is light." (Matthew 11:28–30)

I don't know why but I had a very strong feeling this would mean something to you and that I should jump on e-mail and send it to you. Please don't take that wrong.

All the best!

Eric

I read his e-mail, and when I replied to him, everything came pouring out of me. I told him, "I'm a lost soul, man. My life isn't fun anymore. I asked Jesus into my heart when I was a kid, and I felt something inside of me. I want to get back to that feeling, but I haven't prayed or anything. I feel guilty for not ever going to church. Do you have any advice on where to go from here?"

Eric had some advice. He wrote me back within a couple of hours:

Brian:

Awesome message. I want you to get one concept . . . going to church does not make you a Christian anymore than sitting in a garage makes you a car. A relationship with Jesus is personal. He is your confidant and friend, you can turn to him ANYTIME. He is ALWAYS accepting and no matter what you have done he can release you from any guilt, pain, or shame you have. People in far worse circumstances have turned their lives around and come to know the unconditional love of God! You don't have to make a public spectacle of yourself to accept Christ into your life—you simply need to kneel down right where you are and say, "God, I'm sorry for my sins, please forgive me and come and live within me. Help me walk in your light, read your word daily and rely on you for all my decisions. Let me be an example of you and let others see the change in me because I have made the decision today to give my life to you."

That's it. Then pray as much as you can and read your Bible everyday and make good decisions. Your family will see a change in you, your daughter will see you in a different light and you will have a peace that surpasses your understanding. I would love to come and sit with you to talk more about it.

EP

These messages from Eric were really inspiring, and after reading them, I was almost ready to try Jesus out again, like I had when I was a kid. I needed Jesus to be real. He was my only hope that I had left. I couldn't shake the thoughts: *Is this why my life was so screwed up, because I hadn't done anything with Jesus since that day in my basement bathroom as a kid? Was Jesus calling me back to him so I could start my life over—his way? Would all the addiction, guilt, shame, and pain go away if I gave him my life? Was he giving me the positive thoughts in my mind? Was he the one telling me to leave the band so I could live for him? Could this stuff about Jesus . . . be true?*

I had so much hope, but it quickly faded away when I thought about being a Christian. *You don't want to turn into one of those geeky people you see on the Christian channel on TV*, I thought. *Everyone would laugh at you. Don't be an idiot.* But then I had other thoughts that went the other direction. *What, are you going to stay in Korn, stay hooked on drugs, and die? You going to leave your kid fatherless?* I was also concerned that Doug and Eric would start turning into weird Christians and start bugging me about going to church with them. It just wasn't something that I felt ready for.

There was a battle in my brain—in my soul—and I wasn't sure who I was going to let win. This wasn't the drugs talking to me; this was something different. It was almost like—well, it sounds weird—but it was almost like God and the devil were fighting over my soul. Like it was spiritual fight for my life, but it was up to me to make the final choice.

I had a lot of thinking to do.

Toward the end of 2004, I started having all sorts of weird stuff happen to me. I ran into the guy that I had done speed with when I moved back to Bako with Jennea, and after talking for a while, I found out that he was now an observant Christian. Although he invited me to go to church with him, I never went. Then I ran into an old friend named Bill that I knew when I was a teenager. Back then, Bill was a wild punk rocker who used to go to all the same parties as me and always seemed to get into fights. But now things were different. He too had become a Christian, and he started telling me about God. The whole thing just felt too weird though, and I freaked out on him, calling him a Bible banger and telling him to leave me alone. In addition to these run-ins, one of my neighbors, a mother whose daughter was friends with Jennea, started to ask me if I wanted to go to church with her family. I never took them up on the offer, but it seemed to fit the pattern that had been developing.

Then there was my own daughter. My aunt Deia had started taking Jennea to her Catholic church every now and then, and as a result, Jennea had started to ask me questions about God and Jesus. Questions I didn't have the answers for. When she would ask, I would just point to the sky and tell her that God was too big and far away for anyone to understand anything about him. I felt stupid for not being able to give her a better answer, and I got angry with myself for not knowing more about how to respond.

Everywhere I went, I ran into someone who wanted to bring up Jesus—it was becoming inescapable. And the whole time, I was still thinking about the final choice. The choice I had to make, but all that thinking still did not bring me any closer to a decision.

By November 2004, I wasn't quite done thinking yet, so I grabbed my drugs and hit the road for what would end up being my last tour with Korn. I spent that tour doing drugs and avoiding phone calls from Doug and Eric, since I was becoming increasingly worried that they were going to bug me about becoming a Christian after I responded to Eric's e-mail. As a result, the part of me that was considering Jesus pretty much took a backseat to the rest of me while I was on that tour. I remember having those thoughts of suicide pop up in my head again on that tour too.

A couple of times during that tour, we had to fly to the next show because our buses couldn't make the long drive in time for us to play. Something very strange happened to me while I was on one of those flights. As the plane took off, I had a sort of a half-awake/half-asleep trance. A vision. It was way more than a dream. It was very vivid, like it was really happening. I'd never experienced anything before like that in my life.

In my vision, I was on a different plane, and I was fully awake. It was like a full-on movie in front of my eyes. We were taking off, just like normal, when the plane shifted crazily. I stayed totally calm.

Then the plane shifted again. It tilted.

The plane was going down.

I knew I was going to die.

I heard a huge explosion, and then saw a big cloud of orange fire coming toward me in slow-motion. As soon as it reached me, everything went white. I had been changed in the blink of an eye. No pain.

I was still in motion, moving upward somewhere, and I felt this heavy, heavy peace, like nothing I had ever felt before in my life. I didn't feel the burn or the explosion or anything. I just heard it, and then I knew what was going on.

I had died and I was going to heaven.

I felt so much peace. I felt free. I felt heaven.

I woke up and screamed, "Whoa!" I shook myself, and everyone on the plane turned around to look at me. I thought I'd just been given a premonition of how I was going to die, so I started tripping. I didn't know if that plane was going down or what, but that vision was so life-like that I was pretty convinced I was going to die soon in a plane crash. The plane landed fine, and I started to think about how I'd been doing a lot of drugs, so I wrote that vision off as a weird dream brought on by my drugs.

Something was in the back of my mind, though. I had convinced myself while I was on drugs that whenever I died, I would just turn to dust and sleep forever. But in that vision, I didn't die. I had been charred by the explosion, and I *still* wasn't dead. Instead, I started rising up toward heaven.

What if I had been all wrong about what happens when you die? Was Jesus trying to reach out to me through this vision? Was he trying to tell me something? Was he showing me that I *wouldn't* turn to dust and sleep forever if I died, because there was life after death? Or was he trying to tell me that I needed to die to my way of living so I could be free and have peace in my life? Was he showing me that he was real?

And if that was the case, what did that mean for *me*?

I would soon get all the answers to those questions, but for the time being, I just tried to forget about the vision. At the time, it was too much for me to comprehend.

That tour ended a couple weeks before Christmas, and just after I got home, Eric showed up at my house with an early Christmas gift: a Bible, with my name inscribed on the cover. I was expecting the big Christian sales pitch, but he wasn't pushy at all. He just said, "Brian, if you ever want to talk to me about the Lord, let me know." And then he left. That surprised me. I was sure he would be a pushy Christian now, but he totally wasn't. Even so, I put that Bible away and got back to my drugs. I did poke my nose in it a couple times—I felt kind of drawn to it—but I didn't really understand it, so I would put it back down right away.

Christmas came and went, and I was high the whole time. I felt pretty bad about it though, because I knew Christmas was supposed to be about the Lord's birthday. I bought Jennea's gifts at the last minute on Christmas Eve and wrapped them all night until 6:00 AM, all geeked out of my mind on speed. I think I re-wrapped some of them, like, five times to get them all perfect. I woke Jennea up a few minutes after I wrapped them and watched her open her gifts. Then my parents, my brother, and my brother's family came over, but I was so wrecked from staying up all night that I didn't want to be around them. In the end, I told everyone I was sick and just laid in my bed to get away from them.

A day or two after Christmas, Jennea and I were at the grocery store. I was by the cake section when she came up to me holding a cake. She said with her sweet voice, "Daddy, we forgot to sing 'Happy Birthday' to Jesus. Can we buy him this cake?" I already felt guilty for doing speed on Christmas, not to mention the fact that then, at that moment, I was also on speed. Hearing Jennea say that freaked me out and still does. The Lord was calling me, big-time.

I couldn't resist her pretty eyes, so I told her we could get the cake. We went home, and I put it in the pantry and forgot about it until the next night. Jennea was asleep, and I went to the pantry to get a snack. I saw the cake, and felt that same conviction again, so I picked up the cake and said, "Happy belated birthday, Jesus." And then I ate it.

A few days later, I was up at, like, five in the morning doing drugs, when I got this enormous pain in my chest. It was like a grip on me. I couldn't breathe. I was sweating bullets. Convinced that I was having a heart attack, I staggered to my computer and checked out the symptoms on the Internet. I found a site that listed them, and I had every single one of them, so I called a friend to take me to the hospital.

When I got there, the doctors ran a bunch of tests to find out what was wrong with me. It turned out that I wasn't having a heart attack—but there were all these weird movements on my EKG that they didn't know how to explain. They sent me to a heart specialist who ran all sorts of tests on me, putting me on a treadmill and hooking me up to all kinds of wires and crazy instruments to measure my heart. It turned out that my heart was actually okay, but I knew that I needed to quit meth very soon or my heart might not be able to take it anymore.

That scare was definitely a push in the right direction for me, so when I got home, I called Eric and asked him if he would meet me at a coffee shop the next morning to talk. He agreed, and we set the time.

And then I did a bunch of speed and stayed up all night long—I was completely out of control.

When I got to the coffee shop, I was still pretty tweaked out, but we still sat down in a quiet part of the shop, and Eric started telling me about how Jesus loved me for no reason other than to love me. That it didn't matter what I had done up to that point in my life—Jesus still loved me.

When Eric was done, he suggested that I pray with him to ask Jesus back into my life. I thought, *No way. I've been up all night on speed, and I'm still high right now. If I pray this prayer while I'm high, I'll go to hell for sure.* I figured I had to clean myself up and get off drugs before I could even think about talking to God. Eric led me in the prayer, and I said it anyway, even though I felt a little bit pressured.

As I drove home, I started freaking out. I felt like God was going to strike me down or something for praying to him while I was high. When I got home, I went straight to my bedroom, found the Bible Eric had given me, and started talking to God.

"God, I didn't mean that prayer that Eric pressured me to say! I'm still on drugs, and I know I'm going to do more. Like, today."

I was true to my word, too. I did more drugs that day. And the next. And the next.

A couple of days after I met Eric in that coffee shop, I talked to Doug, and he invited me to go to church with his family that Sunday. I hesitated. I didn't know what to do; I didn't really want to go because I was still on drugs, but something inside me told me I should. So I agreed.

Saturday night rolled around, and I was still a slave to my routine. I put Jennea to bed and started snorting my lines. Stayed up all night. I was still really geeked when Doug, his wife Sandy, and their two boys came to pick us up, so I threw on a hooded sweatshirt to try to hide it. We got to church and headed into the auditorium to go to the service. When the band started playing, all these people around me started raising their hands in the air. Some of them were crying. Some of them started yelling in other people's ears (I found out later that this was how they prayed for each other).

It was all too strange for me and it just freaked me out. These people were weirder than I was—and I had been awake for three straight days.

But something inside me didn't want to leave. I felt a strong sense of love and peace during the music. I stayed through the music, and then the preacher got up and started talking about God. They had these huge projection screens on either side of the stage, and there was a Scripture up there that he was talking about.

It was Matthew 11:28–30. The same Scripture Eric had e-mailed me a few weeks earlier. I just knew they were screwing with my head now. Eric must have told the preacher to put that Scripture up there.

Doug must've told him that I was coming, and so they had set me up. (It wasn't Eric by the way; it was God. It was one way that God used to call me to him. I started seeing that Scripture all over the place for the next couple of weeks.)

Then the pastor said something that really shocked me:

"All you have to do is spend time with God and talk with him and all the burdens you have, all the heavy stuff you're carrying will fall away from you."

Well, that got me really excited inside, because to me, that meant that I could go home, snort lines, talk to God, and then he would take away my addiction. That sounded like it was exactly what I needed, so at the end of the service, when the preacher asked if anyone wanted to ask Jesus into their life, I raised my hand and decided on my own to go through with it. Although I had told God I didn't mean that prayer I said in that coffee shop, this time, I meant it. January 9, 2005, was the day I began my new relationship with Jesus Christ. My life was never going to be the same.

It's worth mentioning that because meth is such an addictive drug, the success rate of kicking it permanently is very low. When you try to live without it, the depression that the drug gives you tells you that you can't—that you must have it to survive. But I knew I *had* to stop listening to the drug and at least give this God, this Jesus, a chance.

Immediately after church, after raising my hand to accept Christ in my life for real this time, I went home, put on a movie for Jennea, and went into my master closet, opened the safe, and grabbed the best bag of meth I had in there. I snorted a line, then sat there on the floor, a rolled-up bill in my right hand, and prayed.

"Jesus, that guy at church said you're real. He said all I have to do is hang out with you and talk to you and that you would take these drugs away from me. Search my heart right now. You know I want to stop. I want to be a good father for Jennea. I tried rehabs and they didn't work, so please take the urge to do drugs away from me. Forever. They've messed up my life. Please make me not want to die anymore, God. I don't want to leave Jennea without a dad. She needs me."

Then I snorted another line.

A couple of minutes later, the phone rang, but I let the machine pick it up. It turned out to be an old friend that I had done speed with a few times in the past. Apparently, he also became a Christian recently and was a member of the church I had gone to that morning. He heard that I had been there and had raised my hand to ask Jesus into my life, so he was calling to encourage me in my new relationship with Christ.

I tripped out.

I'd just finished asking God to help me, and here was this guy on my phone two minutes later. A guy I could trust. I knew that God was telling me to admit my problem to this guy, but I fought it. I didn't want to talk to him—he reminded me too much of speed because I used to do it with him. Besides, I hadn't told any of my friends that I was so hooked on speed. Still, I knew I had to tell *someone* about my addiction, someone who could help me get over it. I was so ashamed. I had hidden this thing from everyone in my life for almost two years; I needed someone I could trust.

About a week later, I bit the bullet and called my old friend D. I told D that I needed to talk. Since my falling-out with his family, we had spoken a couple of times and I had apologized for my past behavior. Because we kind of straightened the whole thing out, I knew I could trust him with my big secret. One day, while Jennea was at school, he came over to my house and I told him about my problem. I took him into my bedroom, unloaded all the meth I had in my safe, and I asked him to throw it all away for me.

When he saw how much was there, his face dropped in disbelief. He almost started crying, he felt so sorry for me. He had never seen such a huge amount of drugs before in his life. He looked at me and said, softly, "What are you doing to yourself, man?"

I didn't have an answer.

Meth stinks, by the way. It smells bad. Especially if you have a lot of it. D was gagging from the smell as he emptied out all of my speed—baggie after baggie getting flushed down the toilet. But he carried on, and soon it was all gone.

I was nervous. I hadn't been able to kick it before. What made me think I could do it now? Somehow, I knew. This was the first time in two years that I felt like I could really quit. And not just speed—I chucked all my drugs; all my Xanax, Vicodin, Valium, Celexa (an anti-depressant I'd started taking). And my beer, too. Beer—the one thing I never gave up for almost twenty years (except for that couple of months after Jennea was born). I gave it up that day.

The thing that tripped me out the most was I didn't have those depressing thoughts like I did before. God was really doing something awesome inside of me. I could feel it. It was time for the next step, so I called my parents and asked them to come over to my house to watch Jennea. I told them I had to go to L.A. for a week for some Korn meetings, but I was really going to check into a hotel in Bako for a week so I could sleep through my drug withdrawals. I got into my hotel room and got ready to stay there until I was clean. That was where I really learned to rely on God.

For the next two days, I only did three things: I ate, I slept, and I prayed. In that hotel room, I was alone with God, and I don't know how he did it, but he got me through those withdrawals fast. On one of those days, I woke up from sleep and started crying tears of hope. I thought I heard God tell me that I was his now, that he was going to use me and my music for his purposes from then on. But by the next day, I had written it off as my imagination. Still though, I was listening to him instead of the drug, and two days later, I was ready to end my seclusion. It was nothing short of a miracle. Usually when someone quits speed, they sleep for two to four weeks straight, but there I was ready to start my new life after only a couple days. I began to feel like a positive person, and I wanted to be around people again. I left the room and started walking around downtown Bakersfield, California, which I had never wanted to do before. It felt so good to be outside in the sunlight.

Right then and there, my drug addiction began to fall away from me. I started talking to God nonstop. I figured that I ignored him for so long that I'd better catch up and make up for lost time. I went back to that church a couple of times after that first week, and I felt like a new man. I was feeling God touch me inside everyday. I would just cry and cry for no other reason than that I just felt loved. I wasn't sad at all. I felt total peace. I had done drugs every day for almost two years, and now here I was, clean for a couple of weeks. I couldn't believe it.

I wasn't the only one who was tripping on it either. D also saw the transformation in me and he could hardly believe his eyes. While he wasn't a Christian, he could definitely tell that something had changed. I talked D into going to a church service with me one night that week, and he agreed. When we were there, I prayed hard for God to reveal himself to D like he had done to me, and after the service, I told D what I had prayed for. I told him to watch for signs from God, because I believed that God would reveal his presence to him—just as he had for me. Once we said our good-byes, we got into separate cars and left.

A couple of minutes later, D called me, freaking out. When he had gotten in his car, he turned the radio on, and it happened to be playing the chorus of "Head Like a Hole" by Nine Inch Nails.

"I'm tripping out right now," he said. "Because when I turned on the radio, I heard the words 'Bow down before the one you serve, you're going to get what you deserve.'"

The timing of turning on the stereo and hearing those words was just too perfect. We both knew it wasn't a coincidence; it was God, speaking through anything that he chose to. After that I had to battle a bit in my mind. I would think, *Maybe that was just a coincidence. Am I getting crazy, here?* But those "coincidences" just kept happening.

Another night after church, I felt like I needed to clean out my tour bags in my closet to make sure I didn't have any more drugs, and sure enough, I found a big bag of meth. I'd like to say that I flushed it, but that would be lying. Like a starving man faced with a peanut butter sandwich, I instantly chopped up that speed and snorted it. There was enough there to last me for a week, and I was determined to make it a week of meth.

I quit talking to God. I put my Bible away. I was going to do the rest of my meth, and then quit for good. In a week or so. I just knew without a doubt that would be my last drug binge ever. I would never do any more drugs, ever again, for the rest of my life. For some reason I just knew this was it. But I figured I had to try to hide from God to go on my last binge.

D was awesome through all that stuff. He encouraged me to stick with my commitment to God—and he wasn't even a Christian. I kept battling in my mind whether all of this God stuff was real or not. D just kept telling me that God was calling me, big-time, that I needed to stick it out and believe that God was real. Perhaps because of his constant support, I hid my last binge from D, too, afraid of showing him my true colors.

During my weeklong meth binge, Korn called a band meeting to talk about the approach we were going to take for our eighth album (what became *See You On The Other Side*). This next album was going to give Korn one of the biggest paydays of our career. Our contract with our record label Sony had just ended and now we were free to sign with any label we wanted, which meant millions of dollars for us. This was a huge factor to my hesitation over leaving Korn. It was probably one of the main things that made me go back and forth about quitting in my head. Little did I know that God was also delivering me from addiction to money too, but it was going to take a bit more time.

I drove up to L.A. at night and met Pete and Jeff in their office. When I got there, I laid it out for them: I wasn't sure I wanted to be in Korn anymore. I didn't mention God—I just said that I wanted to be with Jennea and I didn't want her to be around my rock 'n' roll lifestyle anymore.

Pete and Jeff didn't like that at all, but they encouraged me to go talk to the band, so I agreed. The meeting was scheduled for the next day, and the more I thought about it, the more I realized that I just didn't have it in me. I couldn't look those guys in the eyes and quit. We were a dysfunctional family, but we were still a family, and even though I had been so dissatisfied with the band and with the guys in the band, I still loved them very much, and I couldn't let them down in person. It was just too much for me to deal with at the time.

Instead, I sent them all an e-mail from my hotel, telling them I couldn't tour anymore. Jonathan wrote me back almost instantly. He said, "Head, we love you. We just want you to be happy. What if you write the new record with us, and then we'll find a guitar player to tour in your spot?"

Wow. That was unexpected.

I had all kinds of thoughts going through my mind when I read that. It sounded perfect. I could make music with my friends, be with my daughter, never have to tour, and be a Christian quietly at home. It sounded pretty good to me. I wrote Jonathan back and told him that I had to go home, but that I would think about it and talk to him later. As I drove back home, a lot of stuff ran through my mind. Could I stay in Korn? Could I get that fat payday without touring? Could I actually stay home with Jennea and still do music? It all sounded so good. I stopped thinking and started praying, asking God to show me what to do, and when I got back to Bako, I went straight to Doug's house and asked him his opinion. I figured that, since he was a Christian, he would tell me to quit my evil band or something, but he didn't.

Doug instead told me I should go to the band and see if they would be interested in flipping our music around a little bit to make it more positive. I was talking to him about that idea when I got a message unlike any that I'd ever had:

GO HOME AND WRITE AN E-MAIL TO ALL OF THE KORN GUYS AND MANAGERS AND TELL THEM YOU ARE QUITTING THE BAND AND THERE IS NOTHING LEFT TO TALK ABOUT.

Out of nowhere, I got this strong feeling inside of me. I was hearing God himself. This was way stronger than the words I thought I heard in that hotel room. It was a direct order from God, I could tell. I knew it. I knew it in my heart. For sure.

Without a doubt.

It was such a strong feeling inside me that there was no question at all what I was supposed to do. The back-and-forth that had been going on in my mind for the last year or so was over in a second. And that huge amount of money that I would've received if I had stayed in Korn suddenly meant nothing after hearing God tell me exactly what to do. To me, having that war inside of me finally stop was priceless. I was instantly set free from my double mind and it felt so good. I marched home and did exactly what I had been told. And as I sat there writing the e-mails to each band member, telling them that I was quitting and giving my life to Christ, I started to feel sad about it, but I knew it had to be done. It was done.

I felt free inside. Like I was finally doing the right thing for me and Jennea. However, instead of talking to God about how I felt about the whole situation, I dove back into the last bit of meth that I had. But by then, something was weird about the speed I was doing. I was snorting it, but it didn't seem like I was getting as high as I usually did. I don't know—it was like God was preventing it or something, showing me that he wasn't going to let me enjoy getting high anymore. My mind was clearer. It was time to be done with drugs forever.

Later that evening, I was sitting at my computer and flipping through the pages of my Bible, when I felt a peaceful presence hovering over me. Then I felt something hug me—wrapping around me in an embrace. I don't really know how to describe the feeling, other than to say it was like someone poured liquid love into my body and all around me. I had chills all over my whole body—I had never felt anything like that before in my life. I was caught up in total ecstasy. The high was higher than any drug I'd ever done in my life and I was instantly addicted to it. I looked up and gently said, "Father?" There was nothing there for me to see, but I could feel his presence so strong. It was God.

After an experience like that, you would think that I would have gotten up and thrown away every bit of speed that I had left. I mean, God opened up heaven for me and let me touch him, but after the experience was over, I ended up doing drugs all night. At about five in the morning, I finally fell asleep. When I woke up, I felt an urgency to go to my Bible and open it. As soon as I opened my Bible, I saw a Scripture that completely jumped off of the page and scared the hell out of me. It felt like God literally picked up the words from the Scripture and shoved them in my face.

It was Ezekiel 18:20—The soul who sins is the one who will die.

I instantly felt the fear of the Lord consume me, and I ran into my closet, grabbed the last bit of speed that I had and threw it all in my toilet. After I flushed it, I fell to the ground with my hands in the air and screamed at the top of my lungs,

"I am done with drugs forever! God, did I pass the test in time?"

I've never done drugs or alcohol since, and I never will. Just like that, God took away my cravings. I'm not on any wagon, so I will never fall off any wagon. I'm just done. I had tried to quit alcohol and drugs many times while I was in Korn, but I was never able to do it. On that day all of my addictions (drugs, alcohol, money, pornography) were completely broken off from my life. I knew that, because I now had God in my life, I'd be totally free from my addiction to drugs and alcohol forever. The war was over. I was done running from God. I just wanted to rest in his arms and be free, and that's exactly what I did.

For the next couple of days, God opened up the heavens and let me feel his presence in the same way that he had the night before when I was sitting at my computer. I felt like there were angels all around me, and the Lord was speaking to me through all of them. He helped me understand that he died in my place on the cross two thousand years ago, but he was raised from the dead. Now that I was back with him where I belonged, all of the horrible things I did in my past were forgiven and forgotten. He also guided me with his spirit through Scripture and showed me that everyone who follows Christ will be persecuted in some way. It was like he was asking me if I was up for the challenge. I just remember firmly saying "Yes Lord, I'll do anything for you." I was so wrecked from the heavenly bliss I was in that nothing else mattered.

He spoke with me in a lot of other ways too. On one of those days, I woke up from a nap to see Jennea looking at a book about Pinocchio, and she asked me to read it to her. It didn't take long for me to realize that God was using that story to speak to me. In the story, a toymaker named Geppetto creates Pinocchio, only to find that later on Pinocchio has run off with a bunch of wild boys and started living his life the wrong way. When he eventually runs into trouble and ends up in the stomach of a whale, his creator, Geppetto, saves him from the whale's belly. During the rescue, Geppetto gets hurt so severely that it seems as though he died to save Pinocchio. Eventually he recovers from his injuries and they live happily together.

It was a story that I knew from growing up, but I'd never thought about it on these terms. Given all that I had been through and how I was opening my heart to God, it was very clear he was showing me how I was like Pinocchio, and that Jesus had saved me from my bad choices that led me into the belly of the whale.

As I finished reading the story, I felt so much love from God that I started weeping from the feeling of how much he loved me. I felt more freedom than I had ever felt in my entire life.

In fact, I felt so free that I figured everything in my life was going to get easy from then on.

I would soon come to find I had no idea how wrong I was.

PART II

HEAVEN ON EARTH

EIGHT

I GO PUBLIC

I quit Korn. I completely walked away from everything. Life—as I had known it—was over. That was it.

All at once, I left almost everyone and everything connected to my old life. It was as though my old life had to die so that I could follow the Lord. There was no turning back—and it felt so right. I fell deeply and passionately in love with God, and I made up my mind that he was in control of every part of me from that moment on.

Ever since that intense week when I quit Korn and had my last drug binge, I have dedicated myself to living a life of purity through the power of the Holy Spirit. I'm not saying I'm perfect; I just try as best as I can, but there is no way I could do it with my own strength. The Word says that God is love, and I'm addicted to God's love because he saved me from killing myself with drugs and alcohol. He saved my daughter from losing her dad. He took away all the bad things in my life, and I love him so much for that. He deserves everything that I am, so for the rest of my life, I'm going to try and give him everything that I am. Again, I'm not claiming to be some Holy Roller that lives a perfect, sin-free life.

I screw up all the time, but when I do, I get up, dust my knees off, and keep walking with God.

I was just so deep in the gutter, and the only way I could get out was for God to reveal himself to me, to show me that he's real and that he really loves me. While I was in the worst time of my life, I felt heaven come down and touch me. Because of that, I'll never be the same. It was the most intense feeling in the world. It felt like paradise. It felt like unconditional love. A very intense love that I had never felt before in my life, and that love is what I had been really craving my whole life. The high from all the drugs I did couldn't even compare to the high that God gave me that day.

Since that day, I've been totally living by faith, totally relying on God to fill out every major and minor detail in my life. From growing my faith, to recording my music, to helping me raise my kid, to providing money for me to pay the bills and every other provision I need in life.

Now I want to share with you my victories and struggles about living the *real* Christian life, the real walk of faith. Not the phony stuff you sometimes see on TV, but the type of life where we walk with God the same way the disciples in the New Testament walked with Christ. It's a full-on, risk-filled life that I believe God desires all Christians to live. It's when you completely lay down every part of your life so Christ can live through you.

"I have been crucified with Christ and I no longer live, but Christ lives in me" (Galatians 2:20).

When you decide to trust in God that way, you don't take care of yourself anymore—God takes care of you. It isn't easy at first though; it goes against every logical thing we've ever been taught our whole lives, so some of what I say may sound weird. That's how I felt at first, and I had to overcome a lot of unbelief as I learned about walking this real walk of faith, since it runs counter to the way most people live. To tell you the truth, there are a lot of Christians who don't even live with the Lord this way, either.

Now, I'm not claiming that I'm some super Christian. I'm just a guy who was fed up with living life his own way, so I gave everything I was to God. Everything I had tried up to that point in my life still left me feeling empty, and God was the only one that could fill that empty hole in my soul. I've latched myself on to him and I'm not ever letting go.

All that said, let's back up and talk about what life was like when I first became a Christian. Let's start with this: when God reached down to me and spoke to me, I really believed in him. He was so real to me.

The devil? Not so much. When people would talk about the devil, it just sounded stupid to me. "Ooooh, the devil is gonna come and get me." Real scary, right? But then I had my ideas about the devil changed. I know now that the devil is real, just like God is real.

Soon after my visitation from God, I had a visitation that was either from the devil, or some form of demon. In fact, anybody who sincerely gives his or her life to Christ will come in contact with the devil eventually. I know that sort of thing may sound weird, or even stupid, to some of you, but it's true. Honestly, it sounded weird and stupid to *me*. Until, that is, I experienced it for myself.

After my final drug binge, I was really tired and ready to crash hard. I wanted to crash for a long time. I headed to my room, crawled into bed, and went to sleep almost immediately. I had only been asleep for a few minutes when I woke up, my eyes fluttering open. I looked around and saw the outlines of all the furniture in my room. Everything was still and quiet.

Now, I was really tired when I went to sleep, so there was no reason for me to be awake. At first, I thought I should go check on Jennea or something. I started to get out of my bed when it hit me:

I couldn't move.

I was completely paralyzed.

I. Couldn't. Move.

I freaked. I didn't understand what was happening to me—I just couldn't move my body at all, no matter how hard I tried. I tried to scream out to God, but what came out of my mouth was not my voice. My voice had been replaced by a deep, scratchy noise. It sounded unearthly, like something from *The Exorcist*.

My eyes went wide. I freaked again.

I lay there for a moment, my mind racing, fear pulsating through me. I tried to remember the embrace of liquid love I had felt earlier, but it seemed so far away. This was a totally different embrace. It was an embrace of hate. Of fear. Of some kind of evil I'd never felt before.

And then, just like that, it was gone.

I leapt out of my bed and looked around in disbelief about what had just happened. I had done drugs for years, and nothing like this had *ever* happened to me before, so I knew it wasn't a drug trip. It wasn't just in my head. I could literally feel the evil that was holding me down.

This was real.

I immediately called a friend who knew about this sort of stuff. After talking to him for a bit, he told me that the next time it happened, I needed to do what Jesus had done; I needed to tell the devil to get behind me. Maybe because of all the horror movies I watched, I never believed in the devil or demons or anything like that in my whole life, but now I was being tormented by some kind of evil I had never experienced before. I had Christ in my life now—I wasn't going to let the devil—or whatever it was—push me around. I went back to bed, confident this time that, if it happened again, I would be ready for it.

I soon dozed off, and again, about ten minutes into my sleep, I woke up again, and again, I was totally paralyzed with that same *Exorcist* voice I had earlier, only this time I said in my deep rasp, "Get behind me, Satan."

Nothing happened.

I panicked. Why wasn't it working?

I laid there for a little while, just freaking out inside, fighting this battle in my mind. I was scared to death, but I had to keep believing in God, believing that he was real. Eventually it went away and I went back to sleep, but it happened again. And again. And again. And every time the same thing: I woke up paralyzed, tried to tell the devil where to go, had to sit through mind-numbing terror for a little while, then back to sleep.

Coming off my binge, sleep was the one thing I was looking for, but now this demon or devil was trying to scare me so badly that I wouldn't want to go back to sleep. And if I didn't want to go to sleep, where would I turn? Speed, of course. The devil was using fear as a way to try to keep me on speed. He wanted me to be in bondage to the drug, because if I stayed addicted, I would keep hurting me and my daughter and eventually die.

But these were all conclusions I came to months after the fact. At the time that the situation was unfolding, I didn't have the slightest idea what was going on. All I knew was that it had something to do with God and the devil; the feeling was just too evil *not* to be from the devil. I was touched by good, and then touched by evil—all in the same week. I didn't see either one; I just felt the presence of both so strongly. I had read a little bit about Jesus casting demons out of people in the Bible, so I figured maybe that's what was happening to me, but in truth, I didn't know then and I still don't know today. Only God knows what really went on that day, but whatever it was, it was evil and it had a mind of its own.

The next morning, I called the pastor at that church where I was saved (by the way, if you don't already know this, "getting saved" is a term Christians use when we talk about giving our lives to Jesus), Pastor Ron Vietti from VBF (it stands for "Valley Bible Fellowship," but everyone there calls it "VBF," so I will, too), and asked if he could come out to my house and pray. I was still pretty freaked out about the whole devil thing, so I asked them if they could come over quickly, and Pastor Ron and his wife Debbie showed up a couple of hours later. They went through every room in the house, commanding evil spirits to leave. It was all still pretty strange to me because I had never seen anything like it, but at the same time, I didn't want to get paralyzed again, so I just went with it.

That night, I didn't really feel like sleeping in my bed, because that's where it had happened the night before. I guess I was a little scared that it would happen again, even though Pastor Ron and Debbie had prayed. More importantly though, I knew God was in me; I knew that Christ's power was bigger and better. I kept that in mind as I put Jennea to bed. I laid down with her to help her get to sleep, and then . . .

It happened again.

Total paralysis.

An instant replay of the night before.

But for some reason, I didn't feel any fear this time. Not even in the least. I surprised myself, because I was more annoyed than anything else, but my fear was gone. Instead, I just laughed at how ridiculous it was (at least this time, when I laughed, my voice didn't have that *Exorcist* quality to it).

I laughed again and said, "Let me go, Satan."

Boom. Just like that it was gone, and it's never happened again.

Since I had that experience, I have done a little bit of studying about the devil and demons so I could understand a little bit more about what was really going on with me. I found out that they are spiritual beings (fallen angels) that are very real, very evil, and in the world today. When I was eventually ready to learn all this, it was incredibly eye-opening, but after it happened, I was still a long way away from being prepared to learn about this stuff. Up until I had that experience, I had lived my whole life thinking that everything about the devil was stupid, but my whole belief system got turned around when I experienced it for myself.

That wouldn't be the last time my belief system got turned around.

After those episodes, Pastor Ron and Debbie became friends of mine, and I started hanging out at VBF a lot. The church had its own private school, so I grabbed Jennea out of public school and enrolled her at the VBF school. It was around then that I first told Jennea I had quit Korn to be at home with her and to live for God. She was very excited that I would be able to be with her all the time, and for the first time ever, I felt like a good dad. I had been through so much hell with her, and it felt so good to not only hope, but to know for sure that everything was going to be alright.

In addition to this major change in our routine and Jennea's school, I also started making some lifestyle adjustments. I prayed in front of Jennea and asked God to show her a miracle by taking away my urge to use cuss words. For the most part, he did perform that miracle, but I am human, and I still do slip sometimes. After some reflection, I decided to put all of the gold and platinum Korn awards that were hanging on the walls of my house into my garage. While the idea of those awards made me proud, I needed to move on and it helped not to see that stuff every day. In addition, I also threw away most of the music that I had listened to until my awakening—not because I thought it was devil's music or anything but because I wanted to listen to music that would attract the presence of God since that's all I craved in life.

Also, whenever the doors were open for church, I went. Sunday morning. Monday night. Tuesday night. Wednesday night. I was there three, four times a week. I was doing all I could to get to know God better. Every time I was at a church service, so many tears would fall from my eyes. I've learned that is one of the ways the Lord shows me that he's with me. It's like those are his tears because he's crying right through me.

The thing that totally amazed me is that the place where I felt the presence of God the most was in my own home. I had very intimate moments with God at home, and I quickly realized that God didn't live in a building called a church. Though I didn't fully understand it yet, I was starting to realize that he lived in me and was everywhere that I was. Still, I loved going to church and being around people who had walked with God for a long time. I loved learning things from them.

Around then, God led me to make a list of all the people that I had hurt while I was on drugs so I could contact all of them and ask for forgiveness. He also wanted me to make things right with all of my enemies—even the ones that had done me wrong. That was kind of hard, but God was in control of my life and whatever he said, went, so I made the list. Besides, he showed me that making peace with everyone was part of my inner healing process. And I needed healing deep where I knew only God could reach.

While this healing process was deep, up to this point there was one part of my previous life that hadn't left me: depression. For years, I had been battling depression, even from the early times in Korn. It was this dark, heavy cloud that would come over me from time to time, and just hang there, impossible to escape. I tried to forget about it by doing drugs or drinking beer, but once I became a Christian, I just assumed God would take that depression from me.

He didn't.

For the first few months after I embraced Jesus, I didn't feel that depressed because I was so high on my new life, sort of like I was a newborn baby, but the depression was still there lingering in the background, and little did I know that one day it would come back—with a vengeance.

A few weeks after I got saved, I started to feel like God wanted me to make a public statement about my Christianity, so I asked Pastor Ron if I could give my testimony at VBF during a Sunday service. He told me to pray about it to make sure that was what God wanted me to do; he didn't want anyone pressuring me into it—it had to be my decision. I firmly told him God wanted me to, so we set up a date.

A few days later, I called KRAB-FM, the local rock radio station in Bakersfield. These guys were huge on playing Korn, and I felt like God wanted me to use this station to announce that I was leaving the band, that I had become a Christian, and that I was going to give my testimony at the church. I called up KRAB and wound up going into the studio pretty quickly to do an interview with them. I told them what was going on, and about me giving my testimony at VBF, and that was that.

So I thought.

The next morning, someone from the church called me and said that CNN and MTV had both contacted the church, wanting to do interviews about me quitting Korn and giving my life to Christ. I guess the news of my conversion had hit the Internet, and now people all over the world were freaking out over it. I freaked out, too. I wasn't trying to make a big scene or get a bunch of publicity for myself; I was just trying to follow God, and I thought that, if I could get even a few Korn fans into the church on Sunday, they would have a chance to meet Christ like I had.

Apparently the Korn guys were pretty pissed at me for my announcement because Pete and Jeff were in the process of negotiating a new record deal for them. The *Greatest Hits Volume 1* album we did was the last one on our contract with Epic/Sony Music. Now, Pete and Jeff were in the middle of shopping the band to other labels, trying to get a new deal, and my announcement made it a lot harder for them to do that. While they were talking to record companies, here I was announcing to the world that I had quit the band and was living for God.

But the reality was that I wasn't doing things Korn's way anymore. As much as I loved those guys, I still had to listen to God and try to be completely obedient to him. That's just the way it had to be.

Things started to get crazy in the media, and there was all this fuss about my conversion. I was just sitting at home, tripping out about all this madness, when Pastor Ron called me and said that there was a group of people from the church who were going to Israel the day after I was scheduled to give my testimony, and they had a free extra ticket. He asked me if I would be interested in going to Israel and checking out where Jesus had lived while he was on Earth. I didn't really know if I wanted to, but I felt like God really wanted me to go, so I agreed.

Another thing that happened around this time: I felt the urge to get tattoos of my faith on my body. Now, one thing you need to know is that, while I was a rock star in Korn, I wasn't all tatted down like a lot of rock stars are. I only had four tattoos on my body:

- I had the logo from *Issues* on my arm.

- I had a picture of a guy that had peeled off his skin and was holding it and looking at it. It's like the guy was looking back at his past. This one made me think about starting over when D and I got sober right before I recorded *Untouchables*.

- I had the Korn logo on my lower back.

- I had the word "Jennea" tattooed on my neck, and the name of the child that Rebekah and I gave up for adoption.

That was it. Now though, I really felt like God was telling me to make my body a statement of faith, so I hit up a tattoo place and started getting inked up. For my first one, I went straight for the neck and put "Matthew 11:28" there. It was the Scripture that kept popping up all over the place when I first got saved. "Come to me all who are weary and burdened and I will give you rest." After that, I got the word "Jesus" tattooed on my right hand, with one letter on each of my fingers. I had the tattoo artist write it on my hand so it faced me—I figured that, since I'm right-handed, whatever I was going to do in life, I'd probably start it with my right hand first. I wanted the Lord's name to be the first thing I saw, no matter what I was doing. The next one I got was "Matthew 6:19" on the other side of my neck. That's a Scripture that says not to store up treasures here on earth, but to build up heavenly riches. I got that one because God set me free from my addiction to money.

Sunday rolled around, the day I was going to tell my church—and the rest of the world through the media that had gathered there—that I quit Korn, and was now a Christian. I've got to be honest: I was pretty nervous on that day. Part of that was probably because I didn't know what I was going to say. I had no idea. I didn't write anything down or bounce any ideas off friends. I just winged it. Well, that's not totally true, since I did prepare for it with a lot of prayer. I prayed that God would reveal to me what I needed to say, because there were just so many cameras and people there—even fans of Korn, who'd driven a long way to come see me give my testimony. I also saw some old friends there. Richard, the singer from LAPD, was there, and Korn's wardrobe assistant Lesley. D and his family came (in fact, D's son, gave his life to the Lord that morning). My parents were there, too, and my brother and sister-in-law and a few other relatives of mine. There were also a lot of other people that I used to hang out with when I was a kid there to support me. I took a lot of encouragement from all the support I had there.

On the way to the church to give my testimony, I felt the Lord tell me what he wanted me to say to the people. And what *he* wanted me to talk about, I didn't want to talk about. God wanted me to talk about speed. He wanted me to tell the whole world that I had been addicted to meth, and how he had set me free from that addiction.

Now, up to this point, I hadn't really told anyone other than D about my speed addiction. It was still more or less my secret. While I had told a couple of the guys who were helping me learn more about how to walk with God, they were all former druggies, so I felt I could trust them and didn't feel embarrassed around them.

But there were a lot more than four people in that church. In the end, more than thirteen thousand people showed up to hear my testimony that morning—not to mention the potential millions of others who would hear or see it on CNN, MTV, and whatever other news stations and newspapers around the world that would carry the story.

Basically, God was telling me to tell the whole world that I was a loser.

That was a pretty scary thought, but God reminded me my whole story was about him setting me free from that prison, not about me being ashamed at having gotten in the prison in the first place.

So there you have it. I told the whole world that I had spent almost the last two years of my life addicted to speed. With God's help that morning I confessed my sins to the world. I wasn't even thinking about the fact that most people sort of expect rock stars to be totally hooked on drugs anyway. For me, it was just a truly humbling moment. After the whole thing was over, I was suddenly very thankful that I was leaving for Israel the next day.

While the timing of my trip to Israel could not have been better because of the media circus, I was incredibly excited for my own reasons. I was going to a place that I had never been to, and I had been to a lot of places. This was going to be a different trip though—no band, no guitars, no partying. I was just going as Brian, not as a rock star.

As we were preparing to leave, Pastor Ron got a phone call from his secretary back home at the church. Apparently a camera crew from MTV wanted to go with us on the trip and film everything we did. I guess they were filming a show about spirituality, and they wanted me to be a part of the show. I don't know why, but I agreed. I just felt like it was a chance for me to make God look good, and I hadn't done much of that up to that point in my life. In addition, I was just so amazed at the idea that I would be walking around in the same places where Jesus had walked and I wanted to share that sense of wonder with others

I wish I could say that everything was really mellow on that trip, but I can't. Throughout the whole trip, I experienced mood issues with a lot of anger that came and went. I figured that because I had just gotten saved, it meant I could be totally perfect now. I wasn't going to screw up anymore, or want to do bad stuff. But it just wasn't happening, and my frustration resulted in a lot of anger.

Plus, it didn't help to have that camera in my face the whole time I was there. I had to do an interview at every stop we made, and it was starting to irritate me—perhaps because I could feel the dark cloud of depression waiting just off the edge of the horizon.

Still, I had some very blissful feelings while I was in the Holy Land. A lot of the time, I could feel the Lord holding me, like I had held Jennea when she was a newborn baby. It was this peaceful feeling that God loved me and was taking care of me.

I also wrote some song lyrics while I was there, and I really felt like God was leading me to write a prophetic song to 50 Cent.

One thing to keep in mind before you read these lyrics is that while I believe these words were inspired by God, written through me, to 50 Cent, more importantly I believe the words carry a message to everyone else in this generation, including myself. A message straight to us from God's heart.

Here are some of the lyrics to a song I wound up calling "A Cheap Name":

Wisdom comes through suffering
Tell me why'd you let him give you a cheap name?

It's time to come home
Playtime's over now

It's my world
It's my plan
It's my sea
It's my land
It's my moon
They're my stars
You're my mind
You're my heart
What's your choice?
What's your role?
You're my life
You're my soul
You're my son
You're my seed
We're one love
Come home, please

In addition to writing my first verses of song lyrics, I got the chance to be baptized in the Jordan River, the same river where Jesus was baptized. Now at this point, I had only been a Christian a couple of months, and I didn't know much about how to walk with Jesus. All I knew was that I was supposed to believe, and as a result I had many misconceptions about following Jesus. One area of confusion surrounded the baptism itself. I knew that baptism symbolized being reborn as a new person, but for some reason, I believed that, when I was baptized, every bad thing, every bad feeling, every bad thought was going to fall off of me forever when I came out of the water. I thought that when you go under, you go under as yourself and when you come up, you come up changed. I thought that would really happen: when I went under, that old, angry, depressed me was going to be dead forever. I didn't understand that it was going to be this long, off-and-on, painful process that I would have to go through over the next couple years.

Needless to say, it put a lot of pressure on that moment.

When we got to the baptism spot, there were a bunch of cameras set up from CNN and Fox News and places like that. Not to mention the MTV camera that was already following me around everywhere. It was very nerve-wracking, because that was such a personal moment for me, and to have it all recorded on tape made me nervous, but I felt like God had set it all up. I wasn't ashamed to show everyone in the world how much I loved my God, and how sorry I was for my past. I just went along for the whole press ride.

I had to wait in line to be baptized. About ten minutes. I cried the whole time. Just cried and cried and cried. I was overwhelmed with emotion, and I felt the Lord, right there with me. I was putting my old self to death. A new man would rise out of the water.

When it finally was my turn to be baptized, I started walking deeper into the water, and I was shaking and shivering because it was so cold. Just before Pastor Ron and the other guys dunked me, I asked them to hold me down underneath the water longer than most people because I probably had more junk to wash away. They laughed and agreed. When I finally came out of the water, I felt awesome. The only thing that I really wanted was to go and chill for a bit, but I had to do interviews with the news stations. I even told one news anchor that I believed my evil spirits got washed away in the water. The guy just looked at me like I was out of my mind. And maybe I was out of my mind in some areas, but the one area that I was in my right mind about was getting baptized in the name of Christ; that was the best decision I've ever made.

Despite some of my confusion about baptisms, being baptized was an awesome experience that had an unspeakable impact on my life. I did feel the presence of the Lord change me that day, but instead of being the end, it was merely the beginning. The baptism was just the first step of my transformative process.

Shortly after the group had been baptized, we shared another amazing moment together. In the Bible, after Jesus was baptized, the Holy Spirit (which is one of the three parts of God) came down from heaven in the shape of a dove and descended on Jesus. Not long after our baptism, we were all in a room together, when suddenly another member of the group had his digital camera accidentally go off. He wasn't trying to take a picture, it just happened unintentionally. When he went to take a look at the picture, sitting in the exact center of the frame was a dove. Apparently a dove had flown into the room from the outside at the same moment that his camera went off, and he had inadvertently snapped a picture of this dove that was perfectly straight.

Of course, we were all overwhelmed, because it matched so closely with what God had done for Jesus when *he* had been baptized. We were all convinced that this was how God chose to show us that he was with us. It was an amazing occurrence and it set the perfect tone for the rest of the trip and beyond.

NINE

TONGUES

When I got back from Israel, the only thing I wanted to do was get to know God better, so that I could do whatever he wanted me to do. And one of the ways God speaks to people is through the Bible, so I made up my mind to start devouring my Bible. Unfortunately, though, there were a couple of problems with that plan. The first was that I couldn't sit still long enough to really read the Bible. The other problem was that half the time I didn't understand what it said—sometimes I even had a hard time believing some of the things it said. To solve these issues, I started reading the Bible in little bits, asking God to help me believe and understand it, and spent the rest of my time working on some solo music.

It was around this time that I felt led by God to do a thorough exploration of my master closet, where I used to hide my drugs. I felt as though he wanted me to make sure that there wasn't even one pill or straw left in there. Although I had gone through it before, it was a huge walk-in closet that had two levels to hang the clothes, so it was easy to miss things. On this go-round, I made sure to look through every square inch of that closet and sure enough I found another huge bag of speed I had hidden months before in a first-aid kit of all places. I thought I would never see meth in front of my face again after I flushed it all down the toilet, but there I was, alone at home, with a bag of speed. Bad thoughts instantly came to me.

Nobody will ever know.

I can just do a little bit and then throw the rest away.

One last binge, and then I'll quit forever, no matter what.

"No!" I screamed. I instantly put the bag of meth on the shelf in the closet and walked out of the room and started praying.

"Oh, God, help me! I gotta be done with this shit! I'm not going to be a slave to it anymore! God, please, give me the strength to do the right thing!"

Then I looked at a new tattoo I had on my hand. It was the Scripture reference for Philippians 4:13. I knew that tattoo would come in handy. I quoted the verse out loud:

"I can do all things through Christ who strengthens me."

Suddenly, I felt strong enough to go back in the closet to grab the speed and throw it out. Right then, I found out how powerful the Scriptures really are (Hebrews 4:12). In fact, the Lord gave me so much strength that I got another idea. I decided to get my camera and take pictures of myself throwing the meth away. I wanted to remember this huge day of victory. Up until then, I had *believed* I was delivered from drugs, but that day I really *knew* I was delivered from them. The Lord definitely wanted to show me how much strength he had given me.

After that episode, I really tried to focus on praying, reading my Bible, and writing music. I tried my best to stay out of the press and avoid paying too much attention to the media, since I had heard that a lot of people were making fun of my conversion. While no one was going to say anything that would make me change my mind, it still didn't feel too good to hear negative stuff about myself in the media. Though I knew I would be mocked and it came as no surprise, I had no idea how vicious it would get.

It all began when the lead singer of Tool made a statement that he had given his life to Christ, and MTV called me and did an interview with me about it. I said all this great stuff about how this was exactly what God was doing, and that in the future, there would be a lot of musicians getting saved. In addition, I talked about how beautiful it was that he had gotten saved, and how supportive I was of his decision. Not long after I gave the interview, I found out that it was just a hoax, and I walked right into it. Things got worse when Jonathan started saying some stuff in the press about my conversion. In turn, I said some stuff back about him, and it started to get pretty pointless. After that exchange, I decided then to stay out of the spotlight for awhile.

But behind the scenes, the drama didn't stop. I sent some messed up e-mails to my managers because I was bitter about the exchange. To my shame, I have to admit that I harassed them for a couple weeks, before I could let go of the bitterness. I just had all these emotions going on in me at once, and a lot of them weren't good. I started to feel like I was in competition with my band for some reason, like I was special because God had chosen me or something. As I stepped back and looked at myself, it started to become very clear to me that I had a lot of issues I needed to start dealing with if I was ever going to be a happy person. That was about the time when I realized all of my problems weren't going to just magically disappear right away.

There were other people from my past that I wasn't bitter with though. Around then, a friend suggested that I try to contact Kevin and his family to tell them about the impact that they had on my life when I was a boy. I thought it was a good idea, so the next day I drove to East

Bakersfield and stopped by Kevin's old house to see if his parents still lived there. To my surprise, Kevin's mom, Terry, opened the door. I told her who I was, and of course, she remembered me. She invited me in, and we sat and talked for a while.

Terry had already heard the news that I had given my life to Christ, but what she didn't know was the role that her family had played in my conversion. I told her how I had asked Jesus into my heart after she explained it to me when I was a boy and how that experience was the main reason that I had come to Christ recently. When she heard that, she was just overjoyed; she had no idea that she had impacted me in that way.

It was an incredible afternoon, but our interactions didn't end there. Soon after that, I invited Kevin and his family over to my house for a party that I threw for Jennea. While we were celebrating, Kevin and I hung out for the first time since that summer when we were friends. In speaking to him and his family, it was clear that they were all so happy to know that they had impacted my life in such a positive way.

At the same time that I was reconnecting with Kevin and his family, so many other crazy things were happening. I was so excited to be a follower of Christ that I loved doing anything God told me to do. For instance, I loved praying as much as I could every day, and God would often put certain people in my heart to pray for. One of them was D. I just kept talking to D about how God was so real, and although he believed me, he just wasn't ready to become a Christian. Understanding his reluctance, I kept talking to him about God. One day, I told him an interesting story about one of the pastors at my church, who had actually been sitting on the toilet when he asked Jesus into his heart. My point in telling the story to D was that I wanted him to understand that he didn't have to shout it to the world like I did. He could just accept Jesus quietly, like that pastor had done. Well, one day D told me that he asked the

Lord into his heart while he was taking a dump, and he decided that he wanted to get baptized. It just goes to show you, God really can work through anything.

Shortly thereafter, I met this girl named Ashley who had been a huge fan of Korn and had started coming to VBF. We started talking about the Lord, and she ended up inviting him in her heart as well. After some discussion, she decided that she also wanted to get baptized.

Another person that I had started praying for was my old friend, JC, who I hadn't really spoken to in a while. One day, not long after my trip to Israel, he called me out of the blue and told me he had been arrested for something minor and needed someone to bail him out. While he was in jail, there was a guy who followed him around and talked constantly about Jesus. After listening to him and talking to me, JC decided he wanted to know Christ like I did, so I bailed him out of jail and told him about everything the Lord had done for me. Then *he* wanted to be baptized.

With these three new believers at my side, I called up the church and talked to a pastor named Pastor Jim, and he came over and helped me baptize all three of them in my pool.

But D and JC weren't the only people from my past who were benefiting from the Lord's love. God was also working in Rebekah's life as well. Since we split up, she had been in Hawaii with that skinhead dude, spending most of her time doing nothing, while being massively hooked on speed. One day, she was at the beach, just standing on a pier, when she realized that her life was out of control and she needed help. Rebekah had been raised as a Jehovah's Witness, so she believed in God, and she decided it was time to call out to him. Standing on that pier in Hawaii, Rebekah looked to the sky and said a quiet prayer, asking God to help her.

Sometimes God's help doesn't look exactly like help. A few days later, she got arrested and was placed in a drug rehab program, where she was able to start dealing with her addiction.

Anyway, shortly after I got back from Israel, I felt like I should take Jennea out to Hawaii to see her mother. When we got there, Rebekah told us about asking God for help, and we told her how different our lives were after deciding to give our lives to Christ.

After telling Rebekah all this stuff about our lives as Christians, we asked her if she wanted to ask Christ into her heart like we did, and she said she did. We all said a prayer together, and Rebekah invited Christ into her heart. It was so cool. After all that craziness that Rebekah, Jennea, and I had been through, here we were, the three of us, praying together. It was a complete miracle. When we were finished, she said she felt different—so light, and totally happy. She hadn't felt that way in a long time. I also finally had the chance to apologize to Rebekah for all the pain that I put her through. She apologized too, and it felt good to put all that stuff behind us.

Once Jennea and I returned from Hawaii, I was still praying a lot, and telling God that I wanted to have more of him in my life. I was so hungry and desperate for more of him, and I wanted to get as close to him as I could. It continuously amazed me that the one and only eternal God was so *real*, and he knew who I was. I mean, he actually knew my *name*. I kept begging him to reveal more of himself to me, and he answered my prayers when he had a new friend of mine named Nathan take me to this other church across town named Grace Assembly of God. On the way there, Nathan was telling me about the church, and he said it was Pentecostal.

"Penny who?" I said.

I didn't know what Pentecostal meant, but I was so on fire for God that it didn't matter where I went; I just wanted more of God.

Man, this church was pretty trippy. These people were very passionate about God. It was awesome.

But weird.

And here's the thing that really tripped me out: they all spoke in tongues, or what some Christians call a "prayer language." It's also called "praying in the Spirit" (1 Corinthians 14:4, Jude 20). It's like God giving you the words to pray, even though you don't understand the words (1 Corinthians 14:2).

At first, I found the whole speaking in tongues thing really strange, but I was so excited about God that I started not to care if it seemed strange. To be totally honest, the whole thing completely freaked me out at first because I didn't understand it at all. But I had this burning desire inside of me to find out if it was real, or if it was just a bunch of crap that people did to try and act "spiritual." I stayed through the service, and afterward I met the pastor—Pastor Eddie Summers. Pastor Eddie gave me his number and told me to call him during the week to talk about being *over*-filled with the Spirit. Initially I didn't understand him; I thought I had been filled with the Holy Spirit when I got baptized in Israel. However, I was really hungry for God, so I called Pastor Eddie later that week and took a trip down to his office. After we talked for a while, he prayed with me and asked God to *over*-fill me with his Holy Spirit, suggesting that I ask too.

While I was praying, I felt my stomach suddenly contract, and I knew that God had done something inside me. I didn't know *what*, exactly, but I knew something was different. I felt it. Pastor Eddie started talking about that prayer language, and how God wanted to give me one of my own, so that I could use it to speak to him alone. He showed me in Scripture what it meant (1 Corinthians 14), and after I saw it in the Bible, I believed him. He explained that initially it would sound kind of weird but I would hear syllables come out of my mouth that didn't sound like English or any other language, kind of like a baby trying to talk for the first time. It was very weird to me, but I felt God in it, so I decided to give it a try right there in his office. This was what came out: see-alafol-abaha. It wasn't much, but it was something and we were all stoked. Pastor Eddie suggested that I go home, ask God to give me more words to my prayer language, and wait on him. He would make it grow in time.

So that's what I did. I wanted all that God had for me, and I didn't care what I had to do to get it, no matter how weird it seemed on the outside. And this stuff was weird! But in the Bible, it says that God uses the foolish things of the world to confound the wise (1 Corinthians 1:27), and with that in mind, I was ready to jump straight into the foolishness (but I did have a hard time believing that babbling in some crazy language would actually grow my faith). In spite of my skepticism, it worked, and after enough praying to God, I started speaking in my prayer language. I was talking to God in an unknown tongue, and I could feel it working inside me, building me up (1 Corinthians 14:4, Jude 20). I couldn't explain it; I just knew it was happening.

While I was working on my prayer language, Pastor Ron was really taking me under his wing and teaching me the Bible, becoming a spiritual mentor for me. Once I had my breakthrough with speaking in tongues, I was so excited that I called him up to tell him about it. Unfortunately, he wasn't as excited as I was, and he asked me how I knew that the language I was using was from God. I said I didn't know; I just wanted more of God. No one had ever explained to me that there were different ways to get more of God, and while I was really surprised, I was also pretty bummed.

During the conversation with Ron, I let him know that I had also been studying the Bible with Pastor Eddie, and I was saddened and surprised when Ron told me that if I kept studying the Bible with Pastor Eddie, he couldn't mentor me. While it might have seemed that this was just a ploy to keep me at VBF, I knew this wasn't the case. He just didn't want me to get confused. He understood the risk of having different spiritual mentors, and though he loved me and meant well, he recognized that speaking in tongues just wasn't something they did at VBF.

It was a difficult thing for me to understand, since after all, it was right there in the Bible; however, this experience with tongues became a real introduction into the realities of modern-day Christianity—mainly that there are lots of different kinds of churches called "denominations." Different denominations believe the same basic things but between them there are many little differences that ultimately define what the denomination believes. Pretty much all Christian churches believe Jesus Christ was the Son of God who died for our sins, but beneath that there are a number of other areas where we disagree. One such area is speaking in tongues. Here's my opinion on speaking in tongues: If you want to have the most faith you can have on this earth, learn to pray in tongues. If you find it too weird and you prefer to live a good, quiet Christian life, don't pray in tongues. It's just that simple. It all comes down to personal choice, just like everything else in life. God will love you the same whether you pray in tongues or not.

But when I got involved with God, I didn't know any of this stuff. All I knew was that I loved the Lord and I had learned from the Bible that tongues were a great way to communicate with him. Nevertheless, I had to make a decision about whether to let Pastor Ron mentor me and forget about speaking in tongues, or head to the other church, speak in tongues, and lose Pastor Ron.

It was an incredibly difficult decision. I felt like the Lord had led me to both places, so I couldn't decide *what* to do. For the time being, I decided to stay at VBF. I quit trying to speak in my prayer language, too, because it seemed to be causing all this confusion in my life, and I didn't want to get confused.

But a funny thing kept happening: I kept running into people who told me about speaking in tongues, and how it was the way a Christian could build up his faith. They told me about how speaking in tongues would completely empower me to kill off my old ways, and some random people even sent me a book (through VBF) about praying in tongues called *The Walk of the Spirit—the Walk of Power* by Dave Roberson (which I highly recommend, by the way; you can get it for free on his website). With all of these people calling me toward tongues, I was still confused about the whole thing, and I decided to try some more of my prayer language, since it was becoming clear to me that God wanted me to do it. I started doing it by myself again at home, asking God to develop my prayer language. I figured that, if no one knew I was doing it, then it wouldn't cause a fuss.

During this time, both Jennea and I were growing really close to Pastor Ron and Debbie. She was doing really well in school there, and I was learning about God, but in some ways VBF had begun to overwhelm me. For one thing, there were a lot of people in that church and while that can be a good thing, it also meant that a lot of them were trying to help me in my walk. Everyone meant well, but I was just getting so much outside advice that I couldn't take it all in. In addition, because I was famous, I kind of felt like I was the church mascot and it was making me anxious. The whole situation made me wonder if I was even supposed to be at VBF anymore. I couldn't shake these thoughts, so I prayed about it and the Lord showed me he was leading me to leave VBF—it was just time for me to stay out of churches for a while. The Bible says that the Holy Spirit teaches me all things (1 John 2:27), and it was time for me to go into seclusion so I could learn what God wanted me to learn.

At the same time that I was having my doubts about VBF, I was praying about a much different matter: music. For a while now, I had been thinking about music and the role that it would play in my new life. Now after much prayer, I believed that God was telling me that he was going to use me to do music for him. My music was no longer mine; it was God's. From everything that I was feeling as I prayed to him, I thought that he wanted me to start making music for him as soon as possible. By that same token, I also felt like he wanted to get me out of Bako soon. It just wasn't where I needed to be, and I knew it. The only problem was that I didn't know where to go or what God wanted me to do, so I started praying.

Like I said before: I had given God my entire life. It was up to him to take care of me now. It was up to him to point me in the right direction. I had to rely totally on him. Even so, a lot of my doubts remained. Thoughts would flash through my mind: "What if God only cleaned me up to be a good dad? What if I wasn't supposed to leave Korn?" Some days I just straight-up panicked. It was all so new to me, and I know now that the devil was in the mix somewhere, trying to make me doubt that the Lord was completely in control of my life. Since the beginning the Devil has been trying to make God out to be a liar.

I just didn't understand it. Yet.

The truth was that giving everything over to an invisible God was an incredibly hard thing to do. I was entrusting my life and that of my daughter to a God I could feel, but couldn't see. All I had was his word, his promises, his spirit, and other people who had known him and lived with him for a lot longer than I had. That was all I had to grow in my faith.

But it was all I needed.

I was telling God all the time how much I wanted to live by faith. I was saying, "God, if you want me to do music for you have to get me a manager to help me out." I didn't know how I was going to do the things he had told me to do. I needed help.

Around that time, I got a call from an old friend named "Z." Z used to come hang out at a lot of the Korn shows, and like me, he had committed his life to Christ. In his new Christian life, Z worked at a recording studio and told me I should meet up with his boss, a guy named Steve Delaportes. Well, I just knew I had to check this thing out, because it felt like it might be a divine connection, so I talked to Steve and drove down to Burbank to meet him. When we met, he told me all about this vision God had given him for an entertainment company.

It was an ambitious plan made even better because it was all built around God, but there was more to it than just entertainment. While we spoke, Steve also told me about this ministry he was a part of, a ministry called Good News India that built orphanages for children in the poorest places of India. As he described the ministry, he told me that he would be traveling to India in a few months, and, even though I had just met him, I told Steve that I would be coming too.

Steve didn't know this, but I had recently been praying to God to show me how *he* views the world and see the people that he would be with if he were here on Earth. When I heard about this India trip, I knew God was sending me to his people. Steve, however, had a much different reaction to the announcement that I was coming: he started laughing.

And laughing. He has one of those laughs where, once you get him going, he just won't stop. After he was through laughing though, he agreed to let me come along.

From that first meeting, I really dug Steve a lot. It helped that he'd had a really radical conversion like mine. He had terrorized the world, just as I had, before God yanked him out of that lifestyle, just like he had done with me. It took Steve a little while to quit trying to keep one foot in the world and one foot in Christ, but he eventually surrendered everything he had to God, which was around the time that I met him. I could tell from our first conversation he had so much faith in God and his faith drew me to him. When I saw his faith, it challenged me to trust God a lot more, and he also had more experience walking with the Lord, which also helped me a lot.

Anyway, Steve and I started talking a lot more, and it turned out that God really had brought us together. Because even though Steve had never managed an artist before, we both felt led, like God was calling him to be my manager. We prayed and fasted over it, and within a few days, we knew it was God.

Soon after that, Steve and I decided to become partners in ministry, and under this new partnership, our first order of business was India.

TEN

HEAD HUNTING
IN INDIA

I felt the heart of Jesus the second I stepped off the plane in Mumbai, India. We hit the streets almost immediately, and I was just blown away by how many hungry people there were. It was heartbreaking. I could not believe that more of us Americans were not reaching out to help these people who were in such desperate need. While we were sitting in luxury in America, these people were dying.

Everywhere I looked there were deathly skinny kids running around with no clothes on. Thousands of them. All hungry. A mother was with her son, and someone gave them a bag of nuts or something like that, and they attacked it. I could tell it was the first food that they had eaten in a long, long time. I wasn't the only person who was taken aback by all the suffering; I had brought Jennea with me so that she too, could see how things really are in other parts of the world.

We weren't in India for very long before we started traveling around to the orphanages with Good News India. Before we left for India, God had moved on my heart to donate a certain amount of money toward these orphanages to help take care of these poor kids. When I told Steve how much I wanted to give, he told me I could just pay for a whole new orphanage, and after talking it over, we decided that it would be a good idea to open a new home to show all my fans where my heart now was. Its name would be Head Home, and I instantly got excited at the prospect of helping to ensure that these kids in India were taken care of by all these people who loved them. These kids were so precious, but still so in need of our help. I just kept thinking about how much we as a country could be doing to take care of this problem.

After we first arrived in India, we spent the first few days going to a variety of different orphanages before we went to mine. With each subsequent one that we visited, I became more overwhelmed at the extent of the need and more committed to the cause. When the day came to visit my Head Home, it just so happened that it landed on June 19—my birthday—and at about four o'clock that morning, I was wide awake because of the jet lag, and I suddenly felt the Lord's presence hovering over me in my hotel room, just like I had that one time at my house. He was there, and I started weeping uncontrollably. His presence was just so thick—I couldn't contain it. Then I heard another direct order:

I'M SENDING YOU TO THE UNTOUCHABLES. NOBODY WANTS THEM, BUT I DO. DON'T BE AFRAID.

I had no idea what he meant, but I didn't care. I was freaking out because the Lord had just visited me, and I just wanted to do what he wanted. I got up, showered, got Jennea ready, and met the founder of Good News India, a guy named Faiz (who was an orphan in India as a boy—God rescued him, then sent him back after he had grown up to start this ministry), Steve, and our friend (and lawyer) Greg in the lobby to go open my Head Home. While we were waiting to leave, we got a phone call from this pastor named Tarroon, who was taking care of some of the kids in the orphanages. He said there was a certain tribe called the Loadi tribe that had gotten ahold of him and told him they wanted us to come to their village and talk to them about helping their kids. The Loadi were a very a poor people, but there was something else: they were also murderous cannibals. We all agreed to go, because just before the phone call, I told everyone about that visitation I'd had from the Lord that morning, and the direct order he had given me:

I'M SENDING YOU TO THE UNTOUCHABLES. NOBODY WANTS THEM, BUT I DO. DON'T BE AFRAID.

It all made sense. Still, I thought, "But Lord, these people might eat me!"

Anyway, we took off, and when we got to my Head Home, I saw all these great kids and their house mothers there waiting for us. As we got out of the car, they did this parade/dance/song thing for us that was really cool and unexpected. After that, we saw where they lived, where they slept, and where they ate. We sang some songs to God with them and just had an unbelievable time.

But soon that time was over, and it was time to head into the jungle. Time to meet the Loadi. While I knew God was sending me to the untouchables, I didn't want to take any chances, so we left Jennea at the Head Home to play with all the other kids there. We had already spent most of the day at my Head Home, and I hadn't been scared at all about visiting the Loadi—until we actually started driving to their village. It didn't help that one of the guys with us started talking in this worried voice saying, "These people are ferocious headhunters!"

This was not exactly good news for someone whose name is Head.

Then Tarroon said with a big Indian smile, "If they want to kill us, let them kill us. Then we will be laughing with the Lord Jesus in heaven!" Then he started laughing joyfully at the thought of going to heaven.

I was quietly freaking out. Now keep in mind that I had just gotten saved a few months before this trip, so as these guys were talking about all this, my eyes were bulging out of my head and all I could think was that I couldn't die because Jennea's back at the orphanage waiting for me! I started thinking that maybe that visitation I'd had that morning wasn't from the Lord—it was the devil, tricking me to go there so I could get chopped up for stew on my birthday. Fortunately, I shook it off, and by the time we got there, I was fine.

Good thing, too, because there were about three thousand people there waiting to see us when we showed up. Wearing loincloths over their skinny and malnourished frames, they stood there staring at us and asking how we were going to be able to help their kids. They were sick of seeing their children suffer, and they wanted a better life for them. Seeing all of them in front of me, I began to think about how closely their story matched mine. They were sick of being cannibals, so they reached out to us; I was sick of doing drugs, so I reached out to God. They wanted a better life for their kids, so they reached out to us; again, I wanted a better life for Jennea, so I reached out to God.

They were just like me—only rougher around the edges.

Right when we got out of the car, the man who seemed to be the leader of the group began talking to our interpreter, who translated for us. "He said if you don't help their kids like you say you will, they will hunt down Tarroon and kill him."

See, rough around the edges.

It turned out they were even rougher than I thought. I found out later that some of these people used to go to the orphanages that Tarroon oversaw, beat him up, and steal the children's food. Tarroon would never fight back, though. Instead, he would just tell them over and over that Jesus loved them, but still they continued to come back and steal things. It was from these plundering trips to the orphanages that they had seen the conditions there and knew we could help their kids.

We started the meeting off by giving a little pitch about how we could help their kids. We were all pretty nervous, and one of the elders could tell. In an effort to calm us down, he spoke to our interpreter and said, "We don't even know the number of people we have killed. If we wanted to kill you, we already would have."

Comforting. I took it as the Lord's way of reminding me not to be afraid. Unfortunately, it wasn't really working too well.

We started talking to them about ways we could help them, when suddenly this drunk guy started shouting things at us. I didn't even know they had alcohol there, but it turned out that they make it from tree sap. (Sometimes wild elephants would come by and drink their alcohol, get drunk, and go crazy, ransacking the mud houses the people lived in, and sometimes even killing people.) As the drunken man made a scene, our interpreter explained that the man was talking about how the Indian government had made the same promises that we were making but never came through. As a result, they had to start eating people. They weren't savages—just hungry people.

The meeting ended with no more interruptions, so Steve, Faiz, Tarroon, and I started walking around their property to find a good place to build the orphanage. As we walked, the disruptive man started to follow us and continued to shout. To make matters worse, he was carrying this big tool on his shoulder that they used for hunting. It was a big club with a huge hook on it, sort of like a baseball bat with a hook on the part you hit the ball with. They use the club to kill their prey (animals or humans), then use the hook to drag them home. And now this guy was walking toward us. With his hunting club. It looked like things were going to get rough.

I started praying like crazy. "God, please change this guy's heart. Make his anger go away. You told me not to be afraid, but it's pretty hard right now."

He came closer and closer, and when he finally reached us, he paused for a moment, looked at us, then he burst into tears on Steve's shoulder. He started talking to the interpreter, who relayed his story to us.

"I have five daughters." He reached down, grabbed a handful of sand, and said, "This is all I have to feed them."

This was crazy. One minute, he's looking like he was going to attack us, then I prayed, and the next minute he was crying on Steve's shoulder, pouring out his heart to us.

God is so cool.

Well, we all started crying, of course, because we were just so touched by how much these people needed our help. Really, all they *needed* was love and help. That's it. After that, the presence of God just swept in and took care of everything. At that point in the trip, my whole view on life changed, and God put a deep desire in my heart to help people. The coolest thing was that in the time since we met the Loadi tribe, crime has dropped 90 percent, and today the orphanage is up and running in the Loadi village. Although we have since parted ways with Pastor Faiz and Good News India, that experience was something I will never forget.

By the time that we left India, there was no question in my mind that the trip had changed everything about my faith. Seeing the orphanages and helping the children of the Loadi people were incredible experiences that gave me this remarkable perspective on God and his plan for me—not to mention seeing God's faithfulness come through just in time when things were looking so dangerous. The whole trip inspired me, and my faith in God in such a profound way, that when I got back to the States, I decided to do a little press to make people in America aware of what was going on over there. It was my feeling that perhaps the reason very few people were helping was because no one really knew the extent of the suffering there.

Unfortunately, I quickly found out that this was not the case, and as I discovered not long after my return, many Americans didn't share my concerns. After I got back and spoke about India, I was still so high on my new life with Christ that I thought everyone I spoke to would want to jump on the first plane to go help them—like I did. Sadly, it wasn't so. But still that didn't change the experiences I had when I was there.

Ultimately God changed my heart during that trip, and like all things he does, it turned out that he had a reason. Once again, he was preparing me to turn my life in a totally new direction, and he wanted me to be as ready as possible for what lay in store.

ELEVEN

INTO THE DESERT

When things settled down after my India trip, I took some time to chill. By that point, it was summertime, so Jennea and I had fun just hanging out together. Sometimes she would go over to her nanny's house to hang out, but for the most part we hung out together and had a great time.

During these hot and lazy weeks of downtime, the Holy Spirit really started empowering me to write some more songs. The funny thing was that I was feeling so much peace and love from God, I started writing softer tunes because I just didn't have that same anger in me like I used to when I was in Korn. But as I was writing one day, I felt the power of God's spirit fill me with passion and intensity, and I started screaming at the top of my lungs on one of the songs I was working on. After that day, I threw the idea of doing soft songs right out of my mind. It was clear that God wanted me stay true to my passion for heavy music.

Anyway, I was blown away at how the songs just flowed out of me. Up to that point in my life, I hadn't written full songs by myself before. I had always had a band to write with, but God endowed me with way more musical gifts than I'd ever had up to that point in my life. I was programming the drums, writing the bass and guitar parts, orchestrating the string and choir parts, writing the lyrics, and organizing the song arrangements. It was just amazing.

In addition to writing, I kept heading up to L.A. to talk to Steve about different stuff. The more he and I spoke about my music and my situation, the more I came to see that God was setting me up for a move. Things in Bakersfield had been deteriorating for a while, and ever since I went public with my embrace of the Lord, it seemed like all my friends were either gossiping about me behind my back or trying to shove their noses into every part of my life. The whole situation irritated me.

In addition to these friend problems, God was sending me little signals that it was time for a change. One day when I was backing out of my garage, I noticed a bird that was trapped inside and flying in circles. Jennea and I got out of the car and tried to scare the bird out of the garage, but it kept flying from one corner to the next. We tried to free the bird for a long time but it didn't understand that the door was open for it to fly away. That's when I felt the Lord tell me that he was going to open a door for me to get out of Bako. Still though, I didn't understand how to go about it.

Steve and I bought a recording studio in Arizona, and through all of those things that were happening, I came to see that God was going to send me to the desert, just as he did with the Israelites in the Bible. He made them wander around the desert for forty years in preparation for the Promised Land, and while I didn't know how long I was going to be in the desert, I did know that God was going to send me there to prepare me for his calling and for my life's purpose. I just hoped it wasn't going to be for forty years like the Israelites.

After talking it over, Steve and I developed a plan: Our nanny Connie would homeschool Jennea while I went to Arizona for a few months, and every other week, Connie would bring Jennea out to Arizona to visit me. It seemed like a pretty good plan, but as it turned out, it wasn't God's plan. One day while I was praying, I felt the Lord telling me to get rid of everything in my house in Bako—except for the important things I needed—and then put my house up for sale. In addition, he wanted me to let go of all my friends from Bakersfield, even those friends from my old life who helped me become a Christian. It was his way of telling me to get rid of all the tangible memories of my past and say "good-bye" to the old Brian for good.

I gave Connie a call and asked her to sell all my furniture and possessions because I felt God tell me he didn't want me to go home at all. Then I called a realtor friend of mine named Jeff and asked him to sell my house for me. They did it all. I never went back into that house after God told me to sell it. Connie boxed up the minimal amount of stuff I was keeping and put it in storage for me, while Jeff had my house cleaned and put it on the market.

It was a big change and a hard one at that, so I asked the Lord to give me a sign that this was really him telling me to move and send a buyer really quickly to show me that he was in fact calling the shots. Later that week, the house sold for the exact price I wanted. The people who bought it fell in love with a lion statue that I had in front of the house, and they had to have it. Not long after the closing, I spoke to Jeff, and he informed me that three days after my house sold, the market in Bako had a huge drop-off.

It seemed indisputable that God *was* pushing me out of Bakersfield, but where was he leading me to? I knew God was real, and I kept seeing evidence of that, but even still, I struggled with a lot of disbelief and other difficult emotions. Periodically, my anger was still an issue and my depression was constantly looming in the distance. I had known God for about six months, but walking with him was still really new to me. I loved this new life, but it was hard not knowing what I was doing all the time. Up to that point, I had spent my Christian life just running around everywhere, trying to do things for God. I was running around so much that I never really just sat and tried to enjoy him.

I would pray and read my Bible, but I still felt like God was light-years away sometimes. I didn't really have revelations yet that his Holy Spirit really did live inside me. I had read about it in the Bible and heard all these dudes preach about it, but I had a hard time believing it because I couldn't feel anything a lot of the time. I was running all over the place looking for God, and all I had to do was look inside. I had invited him in there, and ever since that's where he'd been—patiently waiting for me to understand that he would always be with me because he promises never to leave his children.

After I sold my house, I put all the important stuff that Connie didn't sell in storage and waited on God to tell me where to live. I told him I would live anywhere, and I meant it, since at that point, I was living in different hotels. In the end, I could only see two choices: California or Arizona. I really wanted to stick to Cali, so I looked everywhere in L.A., and I even tried to buy a house or two, but everywhere I looked, the doors were shut in my face. It was very discouraging, and I started a new kind of prayer; I like to call it "Freaking out on God."

"God, you told me to quit Korn!" I said. "You told me to go to Israel and India, and to sell my house. Why can't you tell me where to buy a house?"

I finally got tired of the waiting and decided to go to Arizona and get a couple of rooms at the Best Western: one for me and Jennea, one for Connie. While Jennea spent her days homeschooling with Connie, I decided to head into the recording studio for the first time in a year.

From the second that I set foot in that Arizona recording studio, crazy things started happening. While crazy stuff had always happened during Korn's recording sessions, there was nothing that could compare to this. Almost every single day, when I went in, these songs would come pouring out of me. Entire songs would just come out: drums, bass, guitar, strings, choir, lyrics, everything. It was even crazier than before in Bako. I was never able to write music like I did in that season. It was so clear that it was not me; I'd never had a recording experience like it. It was as if God was just downloading these songs inside me.

At first, I wasn't sure where all of it was coming from, but as the songs came out I came to realize that many of them existed because recently I had spent so much time with him. Shortly before I went into the studio, I met a guy named Bob Cathers who was a pretty serious Christian. During our conversations, he taught me all about praying in tongues, suggesting that I pray for hours in tongues, because when you do that, you develop your ability to hear God more clearly in your spirit. I decided to give it a try because I figured that if it didn't work, I'd just stop.

On the whole, I still found the idea of praying in tongues really odd, but the Scriptures can't lie, so I had to follow God's word and not my own thoughts and feelings. Believe me when I say, it was hard. When you pray in tongues, you just sound like a babbling idiot at first, and since your mind doesn't understand what you're praying about (1 Corinthians 14:14), you *really* start to think you're an idiot. However, the Bible says that when you pray in tongues, you're edifying yourself (1 Corinthians 14:4), building yourself up in your most holy faith (Jude 20), even though nobody—not even you—understands you except God (1 Corinthians 4:12). I had to believe the Bible was true, because God can't lie (Hebrews 6:18).

Using tongues, I built my faith and my ability to hear God, and because I chose to pray in tongues for so long, God gave me what I wanted. After I got serious about praying in tongues, a lot of things in the spiritual world started to open up to me. The Bible started coming alive to me in a way that I'd never experienced before. The sections in the Bible that were hard for me to believe just a few months before were starting to become very real. One of the names of the Holy Spirit is called the Spirit of truth, and he was downloading the truth into my Spirit and crushing the "doubting Thomas" part of me. Whereas originally the Bible just felt like an ancient book, now it seemed like God was opening up the door to my spiritual understanding wider and wider. Kind of like a door to another world.

By the time, I went into the studio to record, praying in tongues was a regular part of my prayer routine and these doors were opening up every day. Every morning, before I went into the studio, I spent around three hours with God, praying in tongues. When I finally got to the studio the songs just fell out of me. It was uncontrollable, and even started to happen when I wasn't in the studio. There were a couple of times when I would be talking to someone about something, and God would just speak to me right then and tell me to go to my computer and write a song about what we were discussing.

One time it happened during a conversation I was having with my friend Lisa. We were talking on the phone and she was in the process of explaining how she knew of a child who had a lot of problems and these problems were the parents' fault. Apparently they were kind of mean to the kid, they drank all the time, and they just didn't take care of their child as they should've (sort of how I used to be). During our conversation, Lisa told me how it could be cool to write a song about kids rebelling against the negative things going on in their lives and running to God, so that he could bring healing into their lives like he did for me

After our conversation ended, I didn't think anything else of it until about twenty minutes later, when I heard this music in my head. It was heavy music. And then I heard the screaming words of the chorus:

> *Rebel!*
> *Re——bel!*
> *Your parents have failed you and I'm here to tell you*
> *Rebel!*
> *Re——bel!*
> *The world has abused you and I'm here to choose you!*

(Needless to say, I named the song "Rebel.")

I wasn't even trying to write a song; it just came to me so fast out of the blue. After I thought about it, there was no doubt in my mind that it was from God. The Lord spoke to me through Lisa, using her to trigger the idea for the song.

Something similar happened one morning when I was at breakfast with Steve, and out of nowhere, he said, "Bro, isn't it cool that we're washed by blood?" (He was talking about the fact that the Bible tells us Jesus' blood is the key to salvation. He paid our punishment when he poured out his blood for our sins on the cross. The Bible calls that being "washed by blood.") I responded by telling him that I was really lucky not to be six feet under, and then the conversation moved on.

After breakfast, Steve dropped me off at my hotel, and suddenly, this music came into my head as it had after my phone call with Lisa. I heard the drum parts, the guitars, the strings, the chorus, the verse—

everything. This song was so catchy that I didn't have to go to my computer; I just knew that I would remember it when I went into the studio the next day. Again, I didn't even try to write this song; it just came to me. The chorus went like this:

Washed by blood
From deep inside
You're not a prisoner of your old life
Washed by blood
A brand new start
It's time that I rebuild your heart

So I named the song "Washed by Blood."

That wasn't the only song that came to me at my hotel room. One morning, I opened up the door and saw a newspaper lying on the ground. I picked it up, and that was the first time I saw New Orleans covered by the waters of Hurricane Katrina. Once again, I heard all the music, and then the lyrics for the song "New Orleans" came to me:

Bodies floating
In the streets of New Orleans
What does this mean?
Is the end coming?
People drowning
In the streets of New Orleans
What does this mean?
Is the end coming?

One by one, these lyrics came to me, sometimes in pieces, sometimes all at the same time. After I'd been writing for a bit, God gave me another song called "It's Time To See Religion Die." To me, this song has a few different meanings. For one, it's a song that encourages people to get out of the whole "Sunday Christian" mentality and into the world so God can use them to change the world, to help people understand that God does not live in buildings made by men (Acts 7:48). We are God's building, because he dwells in us (1 Corinthians 3:16).

That's not the only meaning to this song though. Also, this song is for all the people that have been hurt by religion. All of the man-made religion crap in this world has to die. Whether it's Christian man-made religion crap or some other man-made religion crap, it all has to die. It must grieve God's heart when he sees Christians fighting about whose doctrine is right; he doesn't see denominations, he sees one big glorious bride. When Christians argue about doctrinal issues, all he sees is carnal people acting like children. All that prideful, controlling religious crap is what drives young people away from churches, and it has to go. Much of the world's population is under the age of eighteen, and we have to bring the love of Christ to them without all this controlling crap going on. Because, where the spirit of the Lord is, there is freedom.

These lyrics in the chorus came to me rather quickly while I was in the studio one day. It's a "throw your fist in the air" chant:

> *I testify*
> *It's time to see religion die*
> *The truth can't lie*
> *It's time to see religion die*
> *Who cares who's right?*
> *It's time to see religion die*
> *I'll crush the fight*
> *It's time to see religion die*

It is a powerful song and it really came from the heart because God is all about freedom.

Probably the most personal song that touches me the most is a song called "Save Me from Myself," which is something of a roller-coaster ride from my drug use to my suicidal thoughts (with my demonic thoughts telling me to keep snorting more lines) to me crying out to God to save me from myself.

The middle verse talks about me kicking all of my bad habits: drug use, abuse, depression, suicide, and lying. And my favorite part of the song is when I'm screaming to God, thanking him for saving me from myself, and telling him that I'm through with me and am living for him now. The words "save me from myself" were exactly what I needed to scream to God after everything I had gone through up to that point in my life. Here are some lyrics to the verse and chorus:

Another day in life
Which way will I go?
Will I pick suicide?
How do I say no?
The demons are calling me
'Just one more line'
Voices echoing in my head
These thoughts aren't mine
Chop it, snort it
The kid? Ignore it
Life sucks, I'm over it
Save me from myself
Can't quit, I tried it

Your love? Denied it.
Can't fake it
I hate it
Please help me
God, save me from myself
I'm begging you
God, save me from my hell

For a while, I was going through this songwriting phase where I wrote almost a song a day for a couple months, and then, just like that . . . it stopped. I've tried to write songs a few times since then, but I just can't do it; to me, that's just another confirmation God was working and living through me, empowering me to write songs with his Holy Spirit. After the writing process was over, I ended up with about three albums worth of material. While I was writing those songs, we had a guy named Josh Freese come in to record the drum tracks on some of them. Josh isn't a Christian, but he is a great drummer—maybe even the best studio drummer around right now. Anyway, he came in and slammed through my songs, making these beats I wrote sound just awesome. A lot of times, I was still writing songs when he had finished recording, and I really wanted him to stay because he was such a help to the process. He used to joke about me, saying, "I'll be pulling out of the parking lot, on my way to the airport, and there's Head chasing me down the street, holding his guitar and screaming, 'Come back! Don't go! I have another song!' " The truth was that he played a key role in my finding a sound for all those songs. He was such a huge blessing.

I was doing pretty well at that time. But after my run of songwriting when I was writing practically a song a day, I started to feel my depression and my anger coming back. Once the drums were done, I went in to do my guitar tracks, and my temper really acted up sometimes. I would be short with the engineers, and yell at them a lot. In my mind, I didn't want to, but I just had no self-control, so then, in addition to my anger, I had frustration to deal with. In spite of myself, I had a fun time tracking those guitars. I hadn't recorded guitar tracks properly since way back when Korn recorded *Untouchables*. I was so wasted on drugs during *Take a Look in the Mirror* that I didn't even enjoy it. It was so nice recording with a clear mind.

Around this time, I had my first of many real, vivid, prophetic dreams from God. Throughout the Bible there are many stories of God speaking to people in dreams. One of the main reasons he speaks to us in dreams is so that he can bypass our intellect and speak straight to our hearts. My dream wasn't ordinary, and when I woke up, I knew this one was from God. It was incredibly vivid, almost like a movie (like that vision in the plane before I became a Christian) and it totally changed my concept of what dreams could be like.

In that dream, I was with Steve and Jennea in some sort of weird building. Suddenly, I noticed an elevator, and Steve jumped onto the outside of it and held on tightly as it started going up. When Steve started going up, I left Jennea by herself and jumped up toward Steve, grabbing onto his legs. So Steve and I were going up this elevator, on the outside, dangling. We reached the first story of the building, stopped for what seemed like a few seconds, and then we kept going.

And I started to get afraid.

Looking up, I saw that this elevator went *way* high up into the sky, disappearing into the clouds. It was clear that I had a long trip ahead of me and I held on for dear life, because the longer the trip got, the farther the fall was. The elevator stopped on every floor, so it took us awhile to reach the top, but when we got there, we were so high that we were among the clouds.

Once we arrived at the top floor, the elevator started going back down very fast. This part of the trip seemed much more dangerous than going up had, but I wasn't afraid of it. It was actually kind of fun, like a roller coaster, or like one of those death drop rides at Magic Mountain.

When we reached the bottom, I started looking around for Jennea, but I couldn't find her. Somebody told me that she had been very upset that I left her, so she had run away.

I was terrified. I started looking all over that weird building for her, but she wasn't anywhere to be found. She was gone, and my heart was broken.

That's when I woke up. What did it all mean? Over the next couple months, God revealed the meaning of the dream. He showed me that the dream represented the wild adventure that God was going to take us on. He was revealing to me that it would be difficult and a little scary at first, because we were walking completely by faith. It was our job to just hold on tightly to God and trust him completely. Each floor we reached represented the different levels of spiritual growth and understanding that we would receive while walking with God. At the same time, our vertical movement demonstrated how we progressed away from our old ways of doing things, such as trusting in ourselves. We had a lot of pride to get rid of. The achievement of reaching the sky symbolized us reaching enough maturity in Christ that God would release us to his purposes, and then we would go back into the world to bring people close to the Lord like we are.

But there was another crucial message that God wanted to get through to me. At the time I had the dream, I had been working nonstop on my new music. Connie was pretty much taking care of Jennea full-time, and I hadn't seen her much. In that dream, the Lord showed me how I was leaving Jennea out of my new life with God, the same way I had left her out when I was with Korn. But Jennea had been a huge reason why I had left the band. So here I was, doing the same thing with her that I had done while I was in the world, and God was showing me in that dream that Jennea might resent me later in life if I kept pushing her to the side.

Despite the positive aspects of the dream, I felt heartbroken when I woke up, and I knew something had to change. I prayed about it, and within a week, I decided to let Connie go and focus on my relationship with my daughter.

While this dream made me stop and reevaluate my situation, it wasn't the only dream that impacted me. During my time with Korn, I had a dream that reoccurred several times over the course of my ten years in the band, and although I didn't know it then, it turned out to be a dream from God. In the dream, I would be hanging with my friends, drinking and doing stuff that wasn't productive for my life. Then, suddenly, I would get really panicked and run home to my parents as fast as I could, because I had realized I was still in high school and that I hadn't done any of my homework all year long, which meant I wasn't going to graduate. In the dream, I felt like a huge failure. It depressed me. Then I woke up and still felt like a huge, depressing failure. I was disturbed every time I had that dream, but I always wrote it off as nothing more than a dream.

After I got saved, God showed me that *he* had been behind that dream, and that he was trying to send me a message that I was wasting my life. He was trying to show me that if I kept it up, one day it would be too late—I wouldn't graduate into eternity with him. God doesn't make the choice for us—he wants us to choose on our own to live for him. In that dream, he showed me that my fame and fortune wasn't going to get me anywhere at all—I had to choose him.

There's a reason I shared this dream with you. I believe a lot of people—maybe even you—are having God-given prophetic dreams and don't know it. Just like I was. Since those dreams are from God, only the Spirit of God can reveal the true meaning of them. Ask God to reveal to you any dreams from your past that you may have missed. See what he shows you. Because he just might be trying to tell you something.

But it's up to you to listen.

It took me a while to understand that dreams were a totally different way to understand God, and I learned it not only from my one dream, but also from other people that I met along the way who knew about dreams. After we'd been working together for a bit, Steve introduced me to this friend named Benjamin Arde who had these amazingly prophetic gifts. He was thirty-one years old at the time, but he had the wisdom of someone who had been around much, much longer. God called him at a very young age, and he has been living for him ever since.

When I talked to Benjamin, he would tell about some of the things that he had seen, and he always had the coolest stuff happen to him. God gave him some visions of heaven, and he had a lot of experiences where he saw angels. Christ himself even visited Ben once or twice in a vision. I used to joke with him and say, "When is the Lord gonna start giving *me* more visions, Ben? When am I gonna be able to see angels, dog?" He's South African, and he would just say very smoothly, with that accent, "Brian, Brian, Brian. In due time, my friend."

I'm still working on the visions, but Benjamin really does hear from God. He'll tell us about things that are going to happen in our lives before they actually do. One time he even told Steve and me that God was going to replace everyone in our company in the next eight months. Sure enough, eight months later, most of the employees had quit or had been replaced.

Another time, after I had finished writing and recording my songs, Ben had a not-so-good message from God for me. He prayed with me and the Lord showed him that I was going to go through a period of really dying to my old self. God was going to uproot some painful things from my past and replace them with new roots, roots of peace, happiness, confidence, and boldness. But he told me that, before those new roots got planted, I was going to go through a lot of pain while God uprooted all the bad stuff in my past. I was really going to learn what the cross was all about—it was time for me to learn how to suffer for Christ. It's very beneficial for anyone to go through the cross of Christ to get rid of all the pain, bitterness, jealousy, anger, depression, abuse, and all those other ungodly things that we have accumulated over the years. God showed Ben that I was going to just sit there and go through hell a lot of that time. But it wouldn't happen all at once; it would be in stages. And it would all benefit me in a huge way.

Not long after that, I met a man named Kim Clement, who is nationally known for his prophetic gift and is shown all kinds of crazy things by God before they happen. When I sat down with Kim, he explained to me that he had some visions about how God was going to use me to help kids know the true walk with Christ, not the religious walk that pushes so many kids away from God.

While Benjamin and Kim were fascinating, I also learned a lot from a guy named Lance Wallnau who also had a prophetic gift, too. Lance heard something from God about me that I didn't really like at first. He felt like God was telling him that it would be very healing for me to go to my dad and talk with him about my childhood. About his anger, and how it affected me.

The only problem was that I didn't want to do it. I tried to tell myself all that stuff was in the past. I thought it was all "under the blood," as we say, and I couldn't really see what good it would do. I guess my fear of confrontation was trying to kick in again. I decided to check this prophecy out through God and I started praying, asking him if it was for real. Well, actually, I said, "I don't want to do this, Lord. I'll probably just start crying and make an ass out of myself. I'm a grown man. I don't want to bring up the past."

After I finished complaining to him, telling him what was up, I felt like he said:

GO TO THE COMPUTER AND BUY AN AIRLINE TICKET TO BAKERS-FIELD TO TALK TO YOUR PARENTS ABOUT YOUR CHILDHOOD. DON'T BE AFRAID; I WILL BE WITH YOU.

I felt the presence of the Holy Spirit all over me, and I was already weeping uncontrollably. I knew it was another direct order from God himself. He showed me that while my sins were washed away by Jesus' blood, I still had a hard time with forgiveness and suffered from bitterness issues in my heart. The Lord wanted to set me free, but there were steps I had to go through to get that freedom. Understanding what I had to do, I bought the plane ticket.

A week later, I arrived in Bako and went straight to their house. On the morning of the day I was planning on talking to them, I prayed.

"Lord, since you're making me do this, please at least help me not to make a big scene in front of my parents. I'm thirty-five years old. Help me do this like a man."

On that day, I learned another big lesson about God's faithfulness. He was totally with me. It wasn't a big scene at all. In my mind, I had made it out to be this big scary thing to do, but it ended up being really easy. I told my dad how his anger had affected me when I was a boy, and that it had continued to affect me my whole life. Sitting there across from him, I explained how whenever someone raised their voice to me in life, I would get a similar feeling that I felt when I was a boy and he had gotten angry with me. I also told him that when I was a boy, I had felt like something was wrong with me because of his anger. I told him I felt like I hadn't been a good enough son to him. I just laid it all out there.

My dad apologized for everything he had done back then and told me that he loved me very much. He explained how he had problems in his own life that he didn't know how to deal with because his own dad had done the same things to him when *he* was a kid. That anger was a family curse that had been repeating itself in all the generations of our family. By accepting Christ into our family (which my parents did— when I got saved, they started checking out a church to see what I'd gotten into and wound up accepting Christ), the curse was now broken. Now that we were talking about the anger, we were exposing the lies we had all believed about each other. Those lies had no power anymore. It was like God entered our lives and Satan had to leave. The light of Christ exposed all the darkness.

In addition, my mom apologized for whatever she felt she had to, and then I apologized to both of them for all the junk I put them through, like holding bitterness against them inside me for all those years. We all instantly felt like a load was lifted off us; just like that—it was over. And it only took a few minutes. From that conversation on, we have been closer than we ever were before. Similarly, my brother Geoff and I are closer than ever, too. It's amazing how the Lord can restore a family so quickly.

All this stuff was happening around the same time: Connie leaving, recording my guitar tracks, and Lance giving me this prophecy. And that whole time, I was living in this little apartment (we had only stayed in the hotel rooms until we found this place), because I didn't know where the Lord was leading me to live. A couple weeks after my elevator dream, Steve came over to my apartment and said, "Come on, God's gonna give you your house today." I think I asked him if he had backslidden and smoked a joint or something, because I hadn't even been looking for a house, and plus, God didn't let me know where I was going to buy a house—why would he tell Steve? But I was bored, so I went to look with him, figuring it might be fun. The first place we went to was cool, but it wasn't my style. Also, it cost $3 million. I wasn't going to spend anywhere close to that. If I was going to get a house, I didn't need something huge; I just wanted something to fit me and Jennea.

We wound up at this house right next to a mountain, and I felt the Lord say that it was mine. It was like, "Surprise! Here's your house!" I didn't get too excited though. I just figured if it was meant to be mine, then it would be mine. After talking to the realtor about it, I found out that it fell out of escrow about a week before I put my offer in. I took that as a sign from God that the house was supposed to be ours. The sellers ended up accepting my offer, and not long after the closing, I met them.

It turned out they were Christians who had been praying for someone who loved God to buy the house. They loved that house and didn't want to turn it over to someone who wouldn't take care of it, but they were overjoyed at the prospect of us living there.

About a month later, Jennea and I were living in a house again, rebuilding our lives together, by ourselves. We had a blast decorating the rooms and watching our furniture come in, slowly but surely. And I had a great time being a full-time dad, like I was supposed to be. I wasn't relying on my parents or a nanny to watch my kid. Almost all the time it was just me taking care of her: cooking breakfast, making dinner, building my relationship with my daughter and God, taking care of her, taking care of me, and basking in the life that God had led me to.

While I was in the process of buying the house, I had some other financial issues that were occupying my attention. When I quit Korn, I knew that I was done with them, but I thought I still deserved some money, because I was a founding member who had helped build Korn as big as they were. I also owned a fifth of everything Korn owned, including tours and equipment and stuff.

A few months after I got saved, I received a letter from Korn's lawyer saying that they didn't have to pay me anything because they had legally fired me before I legally quit. Since I only told the band and the press that I quit and didn't do anything with contracts, I had opened myself up to that. Still, when I got that letter, I got really hurt, and, to tell the truth, pissed off at them. I felt betrayed (probably the same way they had felt when I quit). In response, I got all my lawyers together and decided to do a big audit. I got kind of suspicious and thought I was going to find out all this stuff in the audit, like maybe that our business managers or our band managers (Jeff and Pete) had been pocketing hidden money or something like that. Really, I just wanted what was owed to me.

I ended up spending almost a hundred thousand dollars on that audit, and it was still going on when I bought that house for me and Jennea. Then one day, I felt the Lord speak to me inside my spirit. He said a few things:

- He told me to stop the audit and forget about any money that I felt Korn owed me.

- He said I was wrong for being suspicious about my managers.

- He said he didn't want me to have any of that money anyway.

- He said that all I was going to do was stir up a bunch of bitterness between me and my former bandmates (bitterness just sucks the life right out of you).

- He said, from now on, he was going to take care of me his way.

What could I do? I had to listen to God.

I called my lawyers and told them to drop everything, which they did, except there was one thing they couldn't drop: the bill. Well, I guess they did drop it. Into my hand to pay it. I was like, "Lord, why didn't you show me this stuff seventy thousand dollars ago?"

He didn't answer.

These legal fees weren't the only expenses that I was faced with. By this time, I had spent a lot of money on my new recording studio and on paying for my engineers and other personnel. In addition to buying that equipment, I also felt moved to give some very extravagant gifts to some different Christian ministries, which was hard for me at first. I had spent years of my life thinking that all those Christian places rip people off (and I'm sure a few of them do). But God sees everything, and he will judge everyone according to what they do, including me. My job is not to question, but to do what the Lord says and cheerfully give the money he tells me to give. If I do that, he'll reward me for my obedience.

Giving money to people and ministries when God tells you to is very important to him. He knows that we work hard to make that money; he knows how much money can mean to us, because most of us spend more time at work than we do at home with our families. But as you give whatever amount the Lord tells you to give, you're showing him that you trust him to take care of your needs. You're showing him that money is not your god. When you give, he sees how much you give as well as the attitude you give it with, and he ends up giving you back more than you gave anyway.

I had always hated the feeling of being poor—like back before Korn, when I sold those stolen drum machines to make ends meet. I hated that feeling, I hated stealing, and I hated being broke. So when I got rich, I was determined never to be poor again. I had to keep making as much money as I could, so I saved a lot of the money I made in Korn; invested a lot of it, too. I resolved to have a big fat bank account forever, so I would never have to worry about money again. It was an obsession. I could never have enough. I always needed more.

You can imagine how I felt when I found out I wasn't going to get money from Korn, and then when I saw my bank account getting lower and lower after buying my house, recording equipment, and giving some money away. I really had to start learning about God's provision, because I was panicking.

I said, "God, look at my bank account! I gotta pay my mortgage! I gotta take care of my kid! This is lower than I've seen it in ten years! Please fill it back up! I gave a buttload of money to those ministries, like you told me to! Where's the return?"

Of course, God was testing my faith and trust in him. He was showing me that he was all I needed. He was letting my bank account get to the point where I *really needed* more money in it to live. It wasn't just a mental, greed thing where I just wanted more money. At that point, I really needed more.

And he put it in there.

From that, I learned that now money comes from wherever the Lord sends it from. He pays me, not anyone else. I can't even tell you how much this flipped my mind. Totally renewed it. God set me free from greed and worry. Because worrying about money is a huge problem for a lot of people. It's stressful. It was for me. Since I started walking with God, I try not to worry about money or anything else anymore. Besides, Jesus says in Matthew 6:25–34 not to worry about our lives. The Lord will take care of us. He wants everyone to live a stress-free, worry-free life.

When God told me to call my lawyers off of the Korn audit, I felt like he wanted me to go the extra mile. I wasn't just supposed to call off the lawyers, I was supposed to call Jonathan.

I had spoken to a few of my bandmates since I left Korn, but not all of them. Shortly after I got saved, David called me and told me he was proud of what I did, which was a great show of support that really made me feel good. A few months later, Fieldy's dad passed away, and I went to the funeral. While I was there, I saw Fieldy, and we had a chance to make our peace.

Still, a long time had passed since I had spoken with Jonathan with whom I had exchanged so many nasty words in the press. When I got a hold of him, I apologized for all the stupid stuff I had said in the press, and he did the same. It was awesome. Short, but to the point.

Similarly I had not really spoken to Munky since I left the band, which was always something that I'd felt bad about. When I left Korn, I'm pretty sure Munky felt like I had left him hanging the most. He and I were tight, since we did all the guitars together and we were generally the two peacemakers. Around the time that I called Jonathan, I also sent Munky a few e-mails, apologizing for leaving the way I did. He wrote me back saying that he loved me and forgave me. That made me feel really good, because I really missed him when I quit.

From talking to all of them and to other people, I've heard that those four guys were closer than ever after I left. In the end, I guess the shock of my departure pulled them together. I'm happy about that, and I'm glad that they're doing so well.

TWELVE

I GO THROUGH HELL AGAIN

Once I made peace with my parents and Korn, I felt that I was ready to go into the studio and lay down some vocals to the songs that I had written. However, it didn't take long for me to realize that singing was going to be a lot harder than I planned. Before I got saved, I was pretty insecure about my voice, but I hid it behind drugs and alcohol. Now that I was sober, I didn't have very much confidence in singing my own songs. I was trying so hard to get the performances down that I stopped letting God do it through me. I had forgotten that this whole thing wasn't supposed to be about me anymore, but I was doing just that: making it about me. I was still trying to be the rock star.

It didn't help that a particular dark, heavy cloud of depression that had been in and out of my life for a while was coming back to me in a big way. Though I had felt my depression looming on the horizon for months, it had yet to really affect my life on a day-to-day basis. But I should have known that it was only a matter of time, and as it turned out the vocal tracks did a lot to push me back into darkness and doubt.

In the beginning of recording my vocals, I was overflowing with anger, which made it incredibly difficult to get anything done. Sometimes I would just completely lose it and smash the computer keyboard that controlled the recording while I was doing my vocals. Other times, I would go home and cuss God out a little. Often the depression got so intense that I felt like I wanted to give up. I felt like I had been abandoned, like I was on my own again and I could feel the darkness of my earlier life closing in on me. I was living the prophecy that Benjamin had given me about completely dying to myself and it was incredibly difficult. What made it even harder was the fact that I was so confused and disillusioned I couldn't even remember the Lord warned me about all of this stuff when he gave me the prophecy. My soul was in complete darkness, and I could barely see God at all. I couldn't understand what the hell was going on with me.

That was a very hard time in my walk with God, but I didn't give up. I didn't understand what was happening to me so I had to learn to completely trust God. I was so used to being totally numb that I didn't know how to deal with the pain I was feeling and asking God to help me through was totally new to me.

One day, I felt so much pain and torment in my soul that I totally lost it and screamed at God.

"Fuck you God!" I yelled.

"I hate you!"

"Get away from me, get out of my life, and leave me the fuck alone!"

"I thought I got saved!"

"Why are you letting me go through this *hell*?"

"Why are you letting me go through this torture?"

I didn't know what I was saying. I didn't know what I was feeling; I didn't even know what I was thinking. But even after I said those horrible things to God, I felt him smiling down on me. He gently helped me understand that I had done a lot of damage to myself over the years, and it was going to take some time to heal those wounds.

The Lord knew it was going to be hard for me to change into the person he wanted me to be, because I was so used to living the total opposite. He had a lot of hell to squeeze out of me, and believe me—when the hell leaves you, sometimes it screams at God on the way out. And when the pain from your past leaves you, sometimes you have to feel it again on the way out. There is nothing we can say or do that will separate us from the Lord's love. I was really bummed out after yelling at God like that. But the truth is, when I accepted Christ, God became my heavenly Father. And if one day Jennea came up to me and screamed at me, "Fuck you dad!" I would still love her the same. And God still loves me the same. Those times really made me thankful that the blood of Jesus covered all my sins and that God would never count them against me.

Those hell times were rough times of deep depression that brought out the worst in me. Besides yelling at God, I would be mean to Jennea. I would think about doing drugs, and sometimes I would even wish I were dead. There were so many nights that I would have bad dreams in which I would go back to Korn on drugs, while everyone laughed at me, saying, "I knew he wouldn't last as a Christian."

Perhaps the most frustrating thing about all of this was that I couldn't control any of it and I couldn't find my faith in God like I had in the beginning. I was going through the things that Benjamin had prophesied for me, but I had absolutely no power over them. It was harder than I could have every imagined. To this day, I still don't understand everything that went on during those times, or what it was all about, but

I remember feeling like God was really mad at me. I know now that it had nothing to do with God being mad at me, but back then I used to wonder why he wouldn't just heal me. I was so confused. Was he testing me to see if I went back to my old ways? I wasn't sure.

I cried and cried, pledging to God never to go back into the world. Begging him to take away the depression.

"God, please stop this pain and depression. I'm sorry for everything I've ever done in my life! I'm so sorry for cussing at you! Please take this away!"

Anything I could think of, I apologized for. I tried making a list of everyone I had hurt and everyone who had hurt me, and I would cry out to God.

"God! I forgive so-and-so!"

"God! I'm sorry I hurt so-and-so!"

"God, I thought I was your son! I wouldn't let Jennea go through this; why are you letting me?"

And then it would go away for a week, but it would always come back.

But then one day I finally realized that screaming at God and begging him to take away my pain wasn't going work. So I completely surrendered myself and stopped fighting him and I asked him what he wanted me to do.

He said:

JUST WORSHIP ME. PRAISE ME AND WORSHIP ME THROUGH THE PAIN.

And that's what I did.

I cried and worshipped the Lord in stillness and silence, listening to worship music and laying on the ground in his presence. It was time for God to do all the work, and it was time for me to be quiet. That's what got me through those dark times. Because God inhabits the praises of his people (Psalm 22:3), and he was right there with me the whole time. He taught me that the only thing I needed to do was be still and quiet while the pain surfaced, and then I could just cry it away. Usually the pain would surface when I was at home worshipping God, but there were times that it would surface while I was out and about in the middle of my daily routines. For instance, I would be driving with Jennea in the car, and I would feel the pain rising and tears would come pouring out of my eyes. But I would cry quietly, hiding my face from her so I wouldn't upset her. Or I'd be in the studio and I would have to step into the restroom to have a good cry. Other times I found myself in public restroom stalls crying for a while too. I would get pretty annoyed when that stuff happened because I felt like a basket case, but I learned to remain silent and not complain to God because I knew that every tear I cried meant more healing for me. It was very hard to cry so much during that season, but God helped me by showing me that the divine light of his Spirit was shining in my soul, burning away all of the junk from my past, and replacing it with the wisdom of his unconditional love—which was exactly what I needed in my soul—love.

As an illustration, he reminded me of what it felt like to walk out of a movie theater in the middle of the day after sitting in the dark for a couple hours. Walking out into the sunlight, my eyes would hurt and burn until I covered them up with my hand. He told me that the light of his presence, which he was shining in my soul, was a similar light, one that created another reason I was feeling so much pain. He also reminded me about all the different people in the Bible who fell to the ground with fear and trembling when they came into the Lord's presence. That understanding completely floored me. I spent so much time screaming at God, or rebuking the devil, when in reality, it was the light of the Holy Spirit that was purging my soul from the impurities so I could be in complete union with God. That understanding made me fall in love with him even more.

But that was not the only encouragement that he gave me; the Lord also said some other things that helped me deal with my suffering. He reminded me of all the pain that he suffered when he was on the cross and how he offered up all of his suffering to his father out of love for him and for us. He showed me that, like him, I too could offer my pain and suffering to the father in the same way he did. I was so comforted with those words, and they continue to comfort me to this day, and whenever I feel bad now, it makes the pain much easier to deal with, because everything I do now is out of love for God.

I've had some of the best times of my life since I became a Christian. I've also been through some of the hardest times in my life too. But I'm sure it wasn't easy for the Lord to get hung on a cross either, and his Holy Spirit will strengthen me with the same courage and endurance as the Lord Jesus had in my time of need.

Those times of worship and fellowship have brought me so close to the heart of the Lord. They made me realize that I can get through anything with him by my side. As time went on, that heavy depression that I had been battling for years finally went away; God completely took it out of me just like all the other things he set me free from. He replaced all those roots of anger and depression with roots of peace and happiness. But I still have bad days just like everybody else. They're not anywhere near as bad as they used to be, but they're still there. In the Christian life, things are not all perfect like some people say they are. It's

kind of like the different seasons of the year. One season you can be seeing, feeling, touching heaven, having all kinds of real encounters with
the Lord, and feeling higher than you ever imagined you could feel. The
next season you might feel so spiritually dry that you're going to crack.
It's just the way it goes. But I've learned that the spiritual droughts are
just as important for my spiritual growth as the times when I'm touching
heaven. It all teaches me to walk by my faith in God's love, not by my circumstances, feelings, or by what I see. The Bible is very clear that Christians are called to be blessed by God, but we're also called to pick up our
own crosses and suffer for our faith sometimes too. The coolest thing is
after we endure our seasons of suffering obediently, God promises that
more of Christ's power will rest on us (2 Corinthians 12:9–10).

I can't sit here and tell you that my life finally ended up perfect after
sticking with God, but I can tell you this: It's all worth it because God is
very real and I can get through anything and everything I have to in this
life, good or bad, because God loves me, and I love God.

Period.

And on top of all that, I can look in the mirror everyday and smile,
because I know that giving my life to Christ was the best decision I ever
could have made for me and my daughter Jennea.

I shared a lot of those gruesome details from my past because I
wanted to show you how much of a monster I was for a reason. I lied, I
cheated, I stole, I abused my wife, I was a horrible father—I was a closet
criminal and the guilt and shame was eating me alive, but I chose to
share those things to prove to you that Christ can and will clear anyone's
conscience from any evil act.

He did it for me, and he will do it for anyone that comes to him
(Matthew 11:28).

I went through a lot of junk to get back to where I belonged, but finally after a lot of work, I'm there. And my main prayer for this book is that it encourages you to seek after a deep and intimate relationship with God.

Take it from me: nothing you chase after on this Earth will satisfy you like a real, everyday, intimate relationship with Christ.

Nothing.

Trust me.

While I was in Korn, I had people waiting on me left and right. Anything I wanted, I got. Anywhere I wanted to go, I went. All I had to do was give the word and it happened. I had the world in the palm of my hand, people, and I have to tell you one last time: there's nothing there. I promise you.

Jesus Christ is the only one that can make you complete.

That's it. That's THE END of my story. Well, on second thought, it's actually only the beginning because my life is just getting started.

EPILOGUE

Have you ever loved someone so much that you would die for them? I'm talking about a love so strong that you would do absolutely anything for that person? Maybe it's one of your parents, or your brother or sister. Maybe it's a boyfriend, girlfriend, or your spouse. If you have a child of your own, you know exactly the type of love I'm talking about. You would do *anything* to keep that person safe, to protect them, or to save them from danger.

That's how much God loves us. His love for us is so deep and passionate—so much deeper than anything we can give to our own loved ones (Romans 8:38–39). God proved that love to us, when he sent his only son Jesus Christ to die a horrible death, instead of us, so that justice would be done and so that we could be reconciled to God through the crucifixion of Christ.

If you ask Christ to be your Savior, you're basically saying, "God, thank you for not punishing me. Jesus, thank you for taking my punishment on yourself." It is an awesome miracle, but that should only be the beginning. Sadly, a lot of people stop right there and go on living for themselves, and while they might be saved and going to heaven, they don't experience the riches of God's fullness in their lives. Those riches are that the eternal realm of heaven is available to us now as we live on earth. We don't have to wait until we die. God will let you experience heaven. All you have to do is ask and keep asking Him.

See, the blood of Christ covers all our ungodliness so that we can go to God boldly in prayer to ask him questions, or just hang out and talk to him like a friend. And that prayer, that first prayer—that is something precious. It is a time when God comes so close to you that, if you're willing, he sends his Holy Spirit to live inside of you. The Holy Spirit is the same spirit that raised Jesus from the dead, and he's the same spirit that took away all the pain in my life. He is very real. The Holy Spirit is God Himself, living in you, speaking to you, listening to you, and showing you how to live this life to its fullest.

He set me free from a broken heart, a broken soul, and a broken spirit; from drug addiction, alcoholism, guilt, shame, abuse, anger, depression, confusion, and on and on. He'll do the same for you if you let him in. A simple, sincere prayer from your heart to God is all it takes to start you on your own personal road to freedom. A prayer like this:

"God, in the name of Jesus Christ, I want to thank you for sending your Son to die in my place. Please forgive me for my past, and help me to believe and trust in Christ. God, please send your Holy Spirit to live in my heart, to teach me how to know you. Thank you. Amen."

That's it. I cut the prayer short, just to give you an example, but you can keep praying for as long as you like, because if you pray in the name of Jesus, I promise you—God is listening. Please don't feel pressured to say this prayer or anything like that. For me, I had to come to a point in my life when I had to decide to be the one to say this prayer, not anyone else. Remember how I said it with Eric, and then took it back when I got home? It's because I needed to come to that decision on my own. I'm not trying to force you into anything here. I don't want you to say this prayer just to say it. My hope is that if you say it, you'll *mean* it; that it will be a sincere prayer to God, straight from your heart.

Once you say it and mean it, all that's left is to pour your heart out to God. Ask him to reveal himself to you. Ask him to baptize you with his Holy Spirit. Ask him to open up heaven to give you a glimpse, because he has invited you (Revelation 4:1). Ask him anything you want. "Because anyone who comes to him must believe that he exists and that he rewards those who earnestly seek him" (Hebrews 11:6). Talk to him like a friend, every day, as much as you can, and he will reveal himself to you. Because now you are a friend, and a child of God. God bless you.

ACKNOWLEDGMENTS

I've never written anything in my life, unless you count the school re-search papers I did to keep my teachers and parents off my back. So I have to give all the credit to God for this book.

Thank you Father for inviting me into your heart and showing me the reality of your paradise, and for your unfailing, unconditional love. Thank you for sending your Son Jesus Christ to die in my place. Thank you Lord for saving me from myself. Thank you for turning all things around for good, and thank you for using me as one of your vessels.

I gotta thank my kid for putting up with her dad while he was going through the roller coaster of emotions—baby girl, God has set Daddy free, and you'll never see that scary guy I used to be again.

Wait up, I gotta thank God again for sending me a couple of guys that could help me make sense of all the scrambled memories from my past, and those guys are Adam Palmer and Jeff Dunn—you're amazing. There's no way I could've done this book without you guys. You were truly hand-picked by God for my book. Adam, thank you for all your sleepless nights and your time away from your family (but you're the one who waited until the last minute).

Matt Harper and everyone at HarperCollins—thank you for

believing in me and helping me get my story out to many people who are in pain.

I also want to thank my family and all of my friends I've ever had in my life, past and present. Especially the ones that went through hell with me and stuck by me even though I didn't deserve it: Mom, Dad, and Geoff; Rebekah; Korn—thank you for allowing me to share the good times and the bad times we had together; Rebekah—I'm truly sorry for everything I put you through while we were together, D—thank you for helping me get off drugs; Kevin, Terry, and the rest of the Amadas—thank you for showing me how to ask Christ into my heart when I was a boy; Benjamin Arde; Ron &Debbie and everyone at VBF; Eddie and Jenae and everyone at Grace; Rex, Jay, Christian, Steve, Doug, Sandy and family, Eric, Sheryll and family, Doug Bennett, Joey, Moses, Connie, and Nathan—thank you for helping me get to know Christ.

I want to thank my friend Lisa, who encouraged me to write this book, even though I wasn't very excited about it at first because writing wasn't one of my specialties. Lisa—you have no idea how writing this book has helped set me free. God has used this book to empty out all the guilt, pain, and shame from my past. Thank you for hearing God and pushing us all to get this book where it needed to be.

I gotta say thanks to my business/ministry partner, Steve Delaportas for going to battle for me. Man, I know for sure that a lot of people would have quit if they had to go through what you go through. Thanks for not giving up.

Thank you to my friend and lawyer Greg Shanaberger for inspiring me to keep going with this book when I thought it ended at my salvation. Some of the best parts of this book are the ones you encouraged me to write.

I want to say a special thanks to all of my fans that stuck by me and didn't ridicule me for my decision to give my life to Christ. Your faithfulness helped me get through a lot of dark times.

I gotta give a shout of thanks to the Montoyas and everyone at Ruby's Tattoo. You guys are all truly amazing and humble artists.

I also want to say thanks to my engineer and friend Carlos Castro. I really appreciate you putting up with my spiritual growing pains, man.

I've done "thank yous" on seven albums with Korn, and I always forgot to thank some people, so I know that I'm forgetting some people right now. I want to cover myself now, so thank you to all the people I forgot to thank.

Okay, that's everyone.

ABOUT THE AUTHOR

Brian "Head" Welch was one of the founding members of Korn. Raised in Bakersfield, California, Head struggled with addictions to alcohol and drugs for much of his life. In 2005, after an intense spiritual awakening, he was instantly delivered from years of substance abuse with almost no symptoms of withdrawal. At that time, he quit Korn to pursue an intimate relationship with God and a closer relationship with his daughter, Jennea. Today, he lives and prays with Jennea in Arizona.